**motivating
people**

MINUTE
10
GUIDE

Macmillan USA
201 West 103rd Street
Indianapolis, IN 46290

Nancy Stevenson

10 MINUTE GUIDE® TO MOTIVATING PEOPLE

COPYRIGHT©2000 BY NANCY STEVENSON

International Standard Book Number: 0-02-863612-0
Library of Congress Catalog Card Number: Available upon request.

02 01 00   8 7 6 5 4 3 2 1

Interpretation of the printing code: The rightmost number of the first series of numbers is the year of the book's printing; the rightmost number of the second series of numbers is the number of the book's printing. For example, a printing code of 00-1 shows that the first printing occurred in 2000.

Printed in the United States of America

Note: This publication contains the opinions and ideas of its author. It is intended to provide helpful and informative material on the subject matter covered. It is sold with the understanding that the author and publisher are not engaged in rendering professional services in the book. If the reader requires personal assistance or advice, a competent professional should be consulted.

Contents

Introduction

Recently I trained a new puppy. All the books I read claimed that, in reality, it's the owner who gets trained not the dog. That's also somewhat true about motivating. This book doesn't tell you what the people who work for you should do; it tells you how, by changing the approach you take, you can inspire your people to respond with more positive and productive behavior in the workplace.

Motivating people involves an interesting mixture of common sense and a deeper understanding of what makes people tick. It's an orchestration of awarding financial compensation, paying compliments, and challenging people to excel. And it's an art that, when performed well, is the hallmark of a good manager.

The difficult and delightful reality is that, as a manager, you work with different types of people. No one magic key opens all their motivational doors. But if you can learn to spot some of the tendencies of different personality types and then pay attention to those signs in dealing with people, alone or in a group, you'll become a better motivator.

In this book, you'll find lots of tips that will help you keep your employees' interest in their jobs alive and well. My guess is that you'll read it through once or twice, find several good ideas to inspire you, then put it on your bookshelf and pull it out now and then to remind you of some specific techniques you can use to address difficult employees or challenging morale situations. After all, an ongoing commitment to being a motivating manager is the real key to motivating people.

Conventions Used in This Book

This book makes use of three icons that help you to find the information you need:

TIP

Timesaver Tip icons give you a different perspective on what has been said to get you thinking.

PLAIN ENGLISH

Plain English icons provide definitions of terms that might be new to you.

CAUTION

Panic Button icons warn you of potentially tricky or dangerous pitfalls.

The Author

Nancy Stevenson has, like a cat, lived several lives to date. She has worked in business settings in the video production, software, and publishing industries. In roles that range from training manager to associate publisher, she has managed a variety of people and projects. In addition, she has been a university instructor of technical writing and a corporate trainer in project management. Currently, Nancy is a full-time author and a consultant to the publishing industry. She is the author of two books on project management, as well as more than a dozen books on computer topics.

ACKNOWLEDGMENTS

I'd like to thank the great team I worked with at Macmillan USA, including my motivating Acquisitions Editor, Amy Zavatto; my meticulous Development Editor, Suzanne LeVert; and eagle-eyed Copy Editor, Krista Hansing; and Production Editor, JoAnna Kremer. In addition, I give my thanks to the many people who made this book happen, starting with Publisher Marie Butler-Knight and continuing through the ranks of editors, production, and manufacturing and sales. Finally, my thanks to my dear friend and fellow author Laurie Rozakis for hooking me up with Macmillan for this project.

TRADEMARKS

LESSON 1

What Motivates People?

*In this lesson, you get a foundation for recognizing what motivates
people and understanding how people's motivations differ depending
on their current needs.*

Let's start with the basics: What motivated you to pick up this book?
You probably want to elicit certain kinds of behavior in someone and
are unable to do it, right? That frustrates you. That challenges you.
Perhaps you're a manager with employees you want to motivate to
enjoy their work more. Or, maybe you have a particular problem
employee who you want to motivate to perform better.

No matter why you bought this book or who you want to motivate, I
won't kid you: Motivation can be a tricky thing. Not everybody is
motivated by the same thing, and what motivates somebody one day
might not motivate him the next. You can never rest on your laurels,
either: One kind of motivation repeated many times becomes the
expected behavior and loses its motivational quality.

In this chapter, I'll provide you with an overview of motivation—what
it is and how it works.

UNDERSTANDING MOTIVATION

The good news is that psychologists who have spent a lot of time
studying what motivates people have come up with some tried-and-
true guidelines that can help you motivate anybody. Throughout this
book I'll provide information on some key theories about *motivation*
that you can use every day.

PLAIN ENGLISH

> **Motivation**   An incentive, an inducement, or a stimulus for action. A motivation is anything—verbal, physical, or psychological—that causes somebody to do something in response.

But no matter how much experts would like to find one key to motivating people, the truth is that individuals are motivated by different things, and what motivates each of us changes throughout our lives. So, using some combination of these theories might be your best bet in motivating people in the everyday world.

EVERYONE IS UNIQUE

Take this example. You have two employees, Ethel and Arnold. They make the same amount of money. They have the same size office with the same size window. They received the same year-end bonus. They were promoted through the ranks at the same speed. You gave them each a nice box of candy for Christmas and complimented their achievements at the yearly employee meeting.

But one is happy, while the other is miserable. How can that be? Simple: Different things appeal to different people, and what's good for the goose is not always good for the gander.

If you're trying to motivate a particular individual, the first piece of advice I can give you is to take a little time to get to know him or her. Notice what seems to make that person happy, excited, bored, or frustrated. And here's a neat trick to use to use whether you're dealing with an individual or a group: Just ask them what you want to know. Nothing is stopping you from sitting down with your employees and asking them to tell you what puts a shine on their shoes and smiles on their faces. Try a few of these questions to help you get a picture of a person's motivations:

- Why did you take this job?

- Why do you come to work in the morning?

- What do you like best about this job?

- What do you dislike about your job?

- What frustrates you?

- What makes you feel valued?

- What was the best job you ever had? Why was it so good?

- What do you expect from a job?

- What do you want from your life a year from now? What about five years from now?

TIP

If you're concerned that people won't answer your questions about their jobs and their levels of satisfaction honestly, make it an anonymous survey. If employees know that you can't identify which comments belong to which employees, they're more likely to respond frankly to questions such as, "What do you dislike about your job?"

People's answers to these questions are likely to be diverse. One employee might come to work for the paycheck, another for the friendships with co-workers, and another for the challenge of taking on difficult projects. One person will thrive on change, while another will be threatened by anything but structure and the status quo.

MOTIVATING PEOPLE IN GROUPS

Does the fact that each individual feels motivated by different things mean that you can't motivate a whole group of employees at once? Not at all. There's nothing wrong with determining what kind of motivation the majority of people in an organization will respond to and then providing that motivation. But the key to motivating a group of people is to vary the kinds of motivation you provide. That extra day off for the holidays might not mean much to that single person without a family to visit and who lives to come in to work. Just make sure that the next perk you offer will be something that he or she will appreciate, such as an employee of the month award that recognizes his or her devotion.

PATTERNS OF MOTIVATION

Luckily, this variety of motivation among people doesn't mean it's random chaos out there. The good news is that there are patterns to what motivates people. Understanding those patterns can help you spot which kind of person or group of people you're dealing with.

MASLOW'S HIERARCHY OF NEEDS

One well-known theory that is very relevant to motivating people is Abraham Maslow's *hierarchy of needs*. If you took Psychology 101 in college, you probably remember this one: People have a hierarchy of needs that determines their actions. These needs start at the most basic level of physiological needs, which include such fundamental requirements as food and clothing. Once those needs are satisfied, people move on to the next level.

PLAIN ENGLISH

> **Maslow's hierarchy of needs**   A theory stating that human beings have an innate order, or hierarchy, for the things they want. When one level of this hierarchy is satisfied, they move on to the next.

Take a look at Maslow's hierarchy, listed from the most basic at the bottom to more advanced at the top:

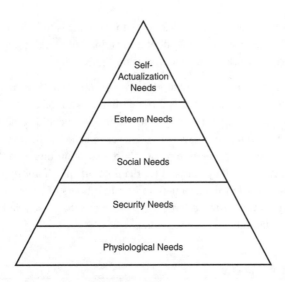

SPOTTING EXAMPLES AROUND YOU

Look around you; if your company is typical, you should see people being motivated at each of these levels:

- The mail clerk who's just out of school wants to pay off his car loan and make the rent every month (physiological needs).

- The single mother/junior executive works to provide medical and insurance benefits for herself and her child (security needs).

- The chatty man in accounting loves the people he works with and lives to organize the football pools (social needs).

- The middle manager works 70 hours a week to earn that next promotion (esteem needs).

- And there's sure to be somebody who does his job not for money, nor for friendship, nor for a fancy title, but because it fits his value system: This is truly what makes his life worthwhile (self-actualization needs).

You can easily use patterns that apply to individuals to identify group needs. Groups of people who do the same kind of work or perform the same level of work often share the same needs.

Here's an example of a way to identify a group need. What motivates employees paid by the hour is different than what motivates salaried workers. For example, let's say you decide to let people go home early on the day before a holiday, but you never indicate to the hourly people that it's okay for them to record those extra four hours on their timesheets so that they get paid for the time off. It's doubtful that the hourly workers felt it was a perk to lose four hours of pay just before a holiday. In this instance, time off was a motivator to salaried people but was a demotivator to hourly employees.

CAUTION

> Avoid using the same motivator over and over again. If you give the team a reward dinner every month rather than when they've performed exceptionally, that night out will become routine rather than motivating.

MOTIVATIONS CHANGE

So that's it, right? Recognize what kind of need motivates somebody to work and meet that need, and you're all set? Well ... no. Unfortunately, it's rarely that simple because people have different needs at different times in their lives.

For instance, once the mail clerk earns enough to cover the rent with money to spare, his physiological needs are met, and he may start to look for more job security (security needs on the Maslow hierarchy). Or, he might jump to the esteem level and look for advancement within the company. Likewise, the person who has had years of promotions and who is respected by her peers because of all her hard work might stop and wonder if all these promotions are worth it if she doesn't have the time or energy to stop and smell the roses. That's when she'll move into the self-actualization phase and perhaps decide to chuck the big salary and impressive title in favor of consulting part-time from home and returning to school to study graphic design.

Not only do people progress through these levels, but they also may bounce back and forth among them. When a major company downsizes, someone who was concerned only with creating a social life at work might jump right back to the security level when he feels his job is threatened.

These different levels of need and the fact that people move among these levels throughout their lives are why it's so important that you get to know the people you work with. Understanding their positions in life and their positions within the company will help you identify the best way to motivate them at any given time.

The same principle of change and growth applies to groups of workers as well. At the beginning of a challenging project, social camaraderie and free pizza might be enough to motivate a group of people to work long hours. But it's likely that this same group will need more substantial recognition and tangible gestures of esteem, such as promotions or bonuses when you're a year into the project. Keeping in touch with the group—and learning to gauge its mood and its needs—is an important part of deciding how best to motivate it over the long haul.

Don't Mistake Your Motivation for Theirs

One of the biggest mistakes managers and supervisors make is to assume that what motivates them is what motivates their employees. That's just human nature. If you're motivated by things that bolster your self-esteem, you just can't imagine someone who simply doesn't need the promise of a raise or a promotion to keep her working. You might just have to walk a mile in her running shoes before you can relate to her perspective.

Here's an example: I once worked in a small company located in an office building with many other small start-up companies. One day, I ran into the office manager from the company next to ours in the parking lot. She had quit and was loading a box filled with her personal belongings into her car. When I asked her why she had quit, she told me that she felt uneasy because her boss kept giving her more responsibility and more promotions. I was amazed: I was craving more responsibility and more challenge from my job after climbing out of the ranks of assistantship, and you couldn't make me go back for all the tea in China.

But this woman had quit to take a job as a secretary, which was actually a demotion from her current position. Her boss hadn't recognized that this employee, though bright and capable, didn't want more responsibility. In fact, she was made insecure by the constant change in her job description and level of responsibility. If her boss had understood that, he might have been able to structure a job to better suit her needs and desires. This was a young, dynamic company, and I have no doubt he could have created such a position. But he couldn't imagine someone satisfied with her position and wanting to stay right there. Because he couldn't understand what motivated her, he lost a good employee.

 TIP

> Use employees' yearly performance reviews as a time to take stock of their current motivational needs. Ask each employee what he or she wants to get out of the job in the next year. If you see patterns of need among several employees, institute policies that address them so that you can motivate all employees to work more productively and be more satisfied with their jobs.

COMMON MOTIVATORS

To help you see the other person's point of view, take a look at this list
of things that stimulate different people to perform their jobs well:

- Money

- Respect

- Challenge

- Structure

- An attractive work environment

- Praise

- Flexible work hours

- Feeling like part of the team

- Wearing casual clothing to work

- Contributing ideas

- Travel

- Not having to travel

- The chance to learn

- Promotions

- Camaraderie

- Recognition

- An award

- Telecommuting

- Free soda in the lunch room

- A discount on company merchandise

- A great retirement plan

- Independence

- Bonuses

- A creative environment

- Being thanked for extra work

- Believing in the job

- Working with other people

- Having set processes

- The boss's trust

TIP

To truly understand how motivations change, just think about what's motivating you to report to work every day. Is what motivates you today different than what motivated you a year ago? Five years ago? Ten years ago?

Now that you know something about the different forms and patterns that an individual's needs fall into, you could probably take this list and slot each item on it into Maslow's hierarchy. Keeping that hierarchy in mind will help you remember that people look for different things out of their jobs, and will help you become a better motivator.

As you read the other chapters in this book, you'll find many suggestions for ways to motivate people. Some will motivate an entire group; others will be more useful in dealing with specific employees. As you choose what you might want to try to motivate your team, keep in mind the guidelines in this chapter, and choose the right motivation for the right people and circumstances.

THE 30-SECOND RECAP

- People are motivated by different needs.

- People's motivations change over time.

- Maslow's hierarchy of needs helps you understand types of motivators.

- Understanding what motivates individuals helps you motivate groups.

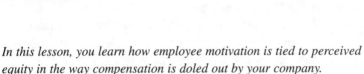

LESSON 2
Take Care of the Basics

In this lesson, you learn how employee motivation is tied to perceived equity in the way compensation is doled out by your company.

Okay, let's be honest. This is probably the one chapter in this book that you feared most. Salaries, benefits—they all add up to you having to pay people more money to get performance. And whether you control the budget or just administer it, you probably don't have money to burn, right?

Most people think that if they can't offer top-dollar salaries or hefty bonuses, people will be lazy and unmotivated. Well, don't worry. You should be less concerned about paying lavish salaries and more focused on giving your employees compensation that you consider fair. Indeed, I'm going to surprise you in this lesson because I believe that the size of the salary or yearly bonus is not always the key motivation for performance or loyalty. Let's take a look.

THE IMPORTANCE OF COMPENSATION EQUITY

In psychology, there is a whole set of *equity* theories of motivation. One key figure in this school of thinking is J. Stacy Adams. Adams states that it is human nature to compare ourselves with others. We compare our looks, our cars, and, most importantly, our salaries with those of our peers. The perception that there's an *inequity* in our compensation at work might seriously impact our motivations for performing.

PLAIN ENGLISH

Equity is the state or condition of being just, impartial, and fair. **Inequity** suggests an imbalance or lack of justice.

Think about it: Does it sometimes seem as if your Human Resources department spends most of its time making sure that no one receives special treatment? It sounds petty at the time: "No, your star employee cannot get comp time for working 30 nights in a row. If he does, everybody else has to get comp time." The result: Nobody gets comp time, and your star performer never puts in another hour of overtime.

Whether it's well implemented or not, there's good reason for this policing of equity. One of the strongest motivational factors in the workplace today is whether employees feel that they are being fairly compensated compared with others in their workplace.

TIP

When you're assigned an employee to supervise, ask your Human Resources department for a salary history. This history can be like a roadmap to employee demotivation if you see that his compensation hasn't kept pace with a coworker's.

REACTING TO INEQUITY

Whenever an inequity exists, either perceived or real, employees react in a few predictable ways:

- **They lower their performance**. "Well, if they're not going to pay me what I'm worth, why should I try so hard? I'll just coast like everybody else around here!"

- **They demand equity**. "I'm going in there to demand that I get what I deserve!"

- **They quit**. "I'm out of here! I'm going to a company that recognizes my contributions."

- **They demand that those they perceive as less valuable produce more.** "Martinez doesn't put in half as much overtime as I do, but he got the same raise I did. I demand that you make him put in the same hours I do!"

- **They realign their comparison process**. "Well, those guys make as much as I do because they're in the Marketing department, and everybody knows that assistants there are way overcompensated. Compared to the assistants in Finance and HR, I guess I'm doing okay."

Another condition that arises when an employee perceives an unacceptable situation is something psychologists call *cognitive dissonance*. This psychological phenomenon occurs when our perceptions of ourselves and the perceptions of the outer world are out of whack. A classic example of cognitive dissonance is the heavy drinker who, knowing that alcohol can be addictive and that his use of alcohol interferes with almost every aspect of his life, still believes that *he* isn't an alcoholic. Reality and his view of himself collide, so he simply denies that the situation exists.

When cognitive dissonance occurs in the workplace, you'll see employees expressing disbelief or denial about a negative situation, or making excuses for themselves or others. For example, despite the fact that an employee *knows* she's doing a fantastic job, her employer fails to give her a raise. It's impossible for her to reconcile the fact that she can do a great job and not get a raise. So, either she's not doing as great a job as she thinks or she will, in fact, somehow get that raise.

However, cognitive dissonance is only a short-term coping mechanism that masks a real problem that won't go away in the long term. The only real solution is to provide the equity employees seek in the first place.

PLAIN ENGLISH

Cognitive dissonance is a condition that arises when there's a conflict between one's perception of oneself and the way the world perceives one.

SETTING COMPETITIVE SALARIES

It's important to understand that wanting to get a competitive salary means more than just receiving a higher paycheck: It is a way for employees to get a sense of their own value. They watch to see whether their input is more or less valuable than that of others as measured by their monetary compensation. They listen at the water cooler when a co-worker gloats about a recent raise, and they wonder what they need to do to earn that same raise. Although salary is just one indicator of their value, it's a measurable one.

TIP

If you have several offices, one key to understanding whether your salaries are fair is to measure them against the cost of living in each area. The salaries for similar positions in your San Franciso and rural Georgia offices might be very disparate. But they also might be fair because of the differences in the cost of living in each area. If a Georgia employee complains when she finds out she's making less than her San Francisco colleague, make it clear how much more it costs to rent an apartment in the Bay Area.

Needless to say, it's very important to understand that salary is tied to an employee's self-worth and motivation; understanding how people respond to perceived inequity is important. But the real world presents barriers to salary equity. Do you recognize any of these common compensation scenarios?

- A lab technician who started 10 years ago at $20,000 now earns $30,000 after receiving regular annual raises. But new lab technicians, right out of school, are getting $35,000 as they come in the door because of current industry demand.

- You spot an employee who is earning much less than others of similar rank in the company and ask the Human Resources department if you can raise his salary by $10,000. Human Resources denies the raise, claiming that giving an employee such a large increase all at once would set a bad precedent.

- Although all employees were promised a minimum 5 percent raise this year, new management has instituted cost savings measures. Those measures include cutting that increase to 2 percent.

All these situations pose compelling challenges for managers. Indeed, it's rare that a manager has the chance to make a clean sweep and totally reset everyone's compensation in a way that he or she thinks is fair. If you find yourself in such a position, I suggest that you try to focus on one employee at a time.

Try this plan for achieving employee compensation equity:

- Evaluate each employee's merits, and help him or her focus on personal growth and performance rather than on what other employees in the company earn.

- Review each employee's salary history and performance evaluations.

- Request information from the Human Resources department on the industry salaries for each position, as well as information about what those in similar positions throughout the company make.

- After evaluating these factors, if you think there's an inequity in an employee's salary, work with Human Resources to find out how much—and how fast—you can adjust it.

- Communicate your findings to the employee in question. As long as he or she knows that you're trying to bring his or her salary in line within the constraints of company policy, he or she probably will appreciate the recognition and effort as much or more than the increase itself.

- If you can't adjust compensation, see if you can offer some other recognition of the employee's value to the company, such as a new job title, a promotion, or a special project assignment.

TIP

> If you can't make changes now but indicate your desire to make things right down the road, employees are often grateful for the attention you're giving them, even if you can't deliver anything tangible right now. Just make sure you *are* working toward eventual change, not just saying you are!

REVIEWING YOUR BENEFITS PACKAGE

Besides salary, you have another weapon when it comes to winning the motivation/self-esteem battle in the workplace: the benefits package. Depending on the size of your company and your role in it, you may or may not have any influence over what these benefits consist of and who receives them.

If you do influence benefits, make sure that you or your Human Resources team knows what other companies in your industry offer and where you exceed or fall short of their packages. Survey your employees about which benefits are most meaningful to them. If you have a choice between offering vision care or dental insurance as part of your medical benefits, give your employees some say as to what they prefer.

If you don't have any control over benefits, you can at least arm yourself with information. Having this information will allow you to use it as an effective negotiating chip in hiring, setting levels of compensation for your employees, and participating in compensation discussions among employees.

You'll need to find out about these items:

- The cash value of your benefits package. Often, the cost of benefits to an employer amounts to about half the employee's salary.

- How your package stacks up against other companies in your industry or area.

- The full range of benefits you offer. In addition to your medical package, be aware of programs such as matching 401(k) funds, tuition reimbursement, and long-term disability insurance.

TIP

An interesting 1949 study looked at what motivates supervisors and nonsupervisory workers. For supervisors, high wages ranked number one, while the amount of compensation merited only fifth place for workers. The lower your wage, the more important job security, benefits, and potential for advancement become in getting you to work every day. Once you've moved up in the ranks, those motivations hold less sway.

PROVIDING SPECIAL FINANCIAL INCENTIVES

Everybody earns a salary, and almost everybody receives benefits (except, perhaps, part-time employees and contract workers). But a bonus is one place that an employer or manager can use his or her discretion.

Companies today are setting up complicated formulas for calculating bonuses. What was once a way for an employer to show unexpected appreciation for excellence has now become a 10-page document that takes an hour to explain in employee orientation.

Still, the way you use bonuses remains an important motivating factor in today's workplace.

A YEARLY BONUS: IT'S EXPECTED

A once-a-year bonus, usually presented around the Christmas holiday season, has become the norm. This is the bonus that is usually based on those detailed calculations just mentioned.

If you're a manager with the power of the purse strings, here are a few things to consider in doling out this money:

- Make sure that people understand that these bonuses are usually determined not only by individual employee performance, but also by how the company or division as a whole has performed.

- If you're allowed to give a higher reward to people who have excelled, use that discretion wisely.

- The way you present the bonus can be as important as the few hundred dollars that goes into the envelope. Take time to present the check, and add a few words of appreciation and praise. An employee often values being singled out for praise more than he does the money itself.

USING UNEXPECTED BONUSES

Expected bonuses are great and can certainly help pay for holiday overspending. But the unexpected bonus—especially one directly tied to performance—may be an even better motivator. Indeed, an unexpected $50 in a weekly paycheck for work well done could be more motivating than a $500 yearly bonus that an employee considers a given. These unexpected rewards simply make people feel special.

TIP

> One motivational experiment isolated two groups of workers. One group was treated differently than other workers at the company; the other was treated just like everybody else. The results? Both groups performed better, simply because they had been singled out to be involved in an experiment, which made them feel special.

Here are some suggestions for formulating an unexpected bonus scheme for your company:

- Provide a birthday bonus for every employee. An extra $100 associated with their special day makes an employee feel special in the workplace, too.

- Tie bonuses to a company's profits. If your company has a remarkable quarter, see if you can share that success with your employees.

- Make use of any discretionary fund for employee entertainment. If you haven't used it all by fiscal year end, ask your management if you could distribute it by giving each employee in your division a $20 bill.

Not all companies will be flexible enough to accommodate these kinds of bonus plans, but it doesn't hurt to ask. The rewards of motivation can be great.

> **CAUTION**
>
> Never, ever promise something you know you can't deliver. The promise of a bonus at the end of a project might act like a carrot to a donkey, but if it never happens, you've done serious damage to that employee's belief in you, your sense of fairness, and your reliability.

NOBODY'S BUSINESS: KEEPING COMPENSATION PRIVATE

Now that you understand how important fair compensation is and have learned a few ways to help manage variables on the salary and benefits front, it's time to figure out how to prevent dissatisfaction over compensation from developing in the first place.

Every business has a policy that discourages employees from discussing their salaries with others in the company. Employers think this is just good management. Employees think that it's part of a bigger plot to keep them from finding out about all the unfair things management is doing to them. The outcome? Telling employees never to discuss their salaries with others often has the opposite effect.

If an employee chronically gossips about salaries and other confidential information, you might be able to bring disciplinary action against him or her, but you'll never be able to stop the occasional confidence.

To cut down on the problems that can ensue from such discussions, make sure that your company has such a policy against revealing compensation and that you explain the policy to employees.

If an employee comes to you complaining about another employee's compensation in relation to his or her own, try these methods of minimizing damage:

- Point out that every employee is different: Each starts at a different salary, which is determined by the general economy, the strength of your industry, and the success of your company *at the time they are hired.*

- Offer that employee an opportunity to change the inequity by meeting certain goals that would lead to higher compensation. Then it's in their control to obtain the higher salary.

- Refuse to compare that employee with the other employee point by point. Instead, move the discussion to a comparison of the employee's performance this year with his or her performance last year. Has there been an improvement? Has that employee received rewards other than an increase in salary, such as a promotion?

In the end, you're better off guarding against the sharing of salary information. If that fails, you should refuse to enter into a discussion about information the employee had no right to in the first place, while attempting to assuage discontent.

COMPENSATION ENVY: KEEPING UP WITH THE JONESES

If you have a Human Resources department, a large part of its role is to keep abreast of current compensation and benefits standards in your industry and geographical region. Work with them to educate yourself on these matters so that you can more effectively manage compensation equity for your employees.

But if you're in a smaller company and don't have legions of HR professionals at your beck and call, you can use other resources to keep yourself educated.

The Internet provides many discussion forums and professional association Web sites dealing with compensation for specific industries. A few good Web sites for general compensation information are these:

- WageWeb, run by Human Resources Programs Development & Improvement (HRPDI), at wageweb.com.

- Society for Human Resources Management (SHRM), at shrm.org.

- Institute of Management and Administration (IOMA). Their Salary Zone, at ioma.com/zone, is particularly helpful.

- American Compensation Association (ACA), at acaonline.org.

If you belong to any professional associations, ask them to forward any of their salary studies, or simply pick the brains of colleagues at association meetings to find out what compensation their companies offer.

TIP

Listen to people you are interviewing for job openings. They sometimes will give you clues as to what your competitors are offering in the way of salaries and benefits.

THE 30-SECOND RECAP

- Concerns about compensation might be less about the total dollars offered and more about the fairness of an individual's compensation in your particular organization.

- It's human nature for people to compare themselves to others, but those comparisons could cause them to spot perceived inequities quickly. Inequity is a great demotivator in the workplace.

- Work within the constraints of your company policies to get and maintain equality of compensation.

- Look for ways other than compensation by which to recognize people, such as changes of title, special bonuses, or assignment to special projects. Singling people out for special recognition goes a long way toward making them feel appreciated.

- Understanding your company's policies and how you compare to other companies gives you the facts you need to deal with unhappy employees.

LESSON 3

Providing a Great Environment

In this lesson, you learn how pleasant surroundings and ergonomic conditions spur productivity.

I observed a very interesting motivational move when I worked for a small video consulting firm. We had just moved into new offices when the owner announced that he was going to buy some artwork to add some visual interest to the place. He went on to say that each of us could choose a picture we would like to display in our own office space. He got a huge catalog of artwork from a framing store so that we could make our choices. The company would pay to have the pictures nicely framed.

We all buzzed around for weeks choosing our pictures and their frames and mattes. We then waited expectantly for a few weeks while the framers did their work. Finally, all the pictures arrived and were hung. They looked great. Although the art soon faded from the topics of conversation around the lunchroom, it gave the office the interest and color it needed, and each office took on a personal look that reinforced the creative atmosphere. This artwork made people feel as if they were a real part of the company, and we all enjoyed coming to work in the morning just that little bit more.

So, if you're looking for a new way to motivate your employees, consider how making your workplace more attractive might motivate better performance.

UNDERSTANDING MOTIVATORS AND DEMOTIVATORS

One researcher of personality and motivation, Frederick Herzberg, conducted a fascinating study from which he devised the concept of *maintenance factors* on the job. Herzberg asked thousands of people to talk about both moments when they felt good about their work and moments when they felt bad.

PLAIN ENGLISH

> **Maintenance factors**   Things about a business that contribute to a healthy business climate, but that do not cause it. For example, a clean lunchroom may not motivate good performance, but if it's not clean, people will complain about it. In that sense, cleaning the lunchroom becomes a maintenance factor.

Out of that study came two lists: a list of things that satisfied people, and a list of things that dissatisfied people. Now you might assume that these lists would consist of opposites: What satisfies a person would be to have chance for advancement, and what dissatisfies that same person would be lack of opportunity. But that wasn't the case— in fact, there were hardly any matches at all!

Look at the top six items on each of these lists:

Satisfiers

- Achievement
- Recognition
- The work itself
- Responsibility
- Advancement
- Growth

Dissatisfiers

- Company policy and administration
- Supervision
- Relationship with supervisor
- Working conditions
- Relationships with peers
- Relationships with subordinates

Here's the conclusion Herzberg reached from this information: What it takes to motivate an employee is different from what it takes to build a complaint-free workplace. Although providing nice working conditions might prevent people from becoming completely dissatisfied, this benefit might not result in complete satisfaction, either. Even more important, it might not be a motivation for employees to perform or to excel.

TIP

> Many companies find it useful to have outside agencies perform satisfaction surveys. These companies tally anonymous results, giving an overall picture of why employees are satisfied and why they are dissatisfied.

Think about this result for a moment and apply it to your own experience. Was your favorite job your favorite because of the company policies, or because you consistently received recognition for your efforts? Although a stingy company policy about comp time might have grated on your nerves, it's doubtful that a fair comp time policy would rank up there with recognition of your contributions when it came to motivating you to work hard. Listen to the people in your office. You'll probably find that they complain most about things like the lack of parking spaces, bad coffee, the vacation policy, and the temperature of their offices. Solve those problems, and you might keep your workers from staging an in-office revolution—but you probably won't have a motivated workforce.

So, is it worth dealing with the bad coffee situation? Yes! The better coffee will not necessarily affect performance, but your willingness to listen and then to take action will have meaning for your employees. Furthermore, by providing the finest Colombian blend instead of instant coffee, you eliminate a source of discontent, one that could be demotivating people in the workplace.

DESIGNING AN INTERESTING WORKSPACE

As you can see, this chapter is about the flip side of motivation: demotivation. Getting rid of things that demotivate people might not motivate them, but it helps you get past the more minor complaints about the lousy lighting and lack of parking spaces to find out what will really motivate workers, such as job growth and advancement.

When it comes to eliminating demotivators, one good place to start is with the general appearance of your workplace. I've often been amazed at the number of businesses I've visited that haven't had a single picture hanging on the walls. I've even worked at companies where displaying anything personal in a cubicle was against policy. Now, I realize that you have to work within the parameters of your own organization, but try taking the following inventory of your workplace to see how you stack up.

At my company, we ...

- Have artwork on display (and not just in the conference room or executive offices).

- Have workspaces with adequate daylight as well as artificial lighting.

- Allow workers to display personal items in their workspace.

- Have live plants around the work area.

- Use a color besides bright white or industrial green on some walls.

What about your workplace? If you weren't able to check at least three of these items as applicable to your company, this chapter is for you!

TIP

Been in your workplace so long you can't see it for the trees? How about bringing a friend or your spouse in and getting their reactions about whether it could use another coat of paint?

As you begin to institute some of the changes suggested here, keep in mind that the display of art and personal items will have its limits. Pictures that are offensive to some people, such as male or female pin-ups, are a no-no. Even cartoons or jokes that have sexual undertones posted on a bulletin board might be a problem. And, needless to say, racist and sexist commentary—even if part of a "joke"—is wrong in any context.

CAUTION

Check with your Human Resources department to learn about some of the limits your company's sexual harassment and other policies might impose on your proposed changes.

THE COLOR ADVANTAGE

Many studies show that color affects mood and that using color wisely can help produce an atmosphere in which motivation, concentration, learning, and retention flourish. For example, lack of vivid color creates boredom, while too much color variation overstimulates people. Too much of any one color makes people irritable and impairs their ability to concentrate.

TIP

> Ever hear the phrase "waiting in the green room"? A green room is where performers wait when they're not onstage. These rooms are traditionally green because green induces relaxation and soothes the performers' eyes, which can be strained by spotlights on stage.

Use this list to help you understand how different colors impact people and their moods:

- Green relieves stress and calms people.

- Blue is another calming color, said to help resolve conflict.

- Red encourages alertness and mental clarity, but in vibrant shades it also can make people slightly edgy.

- Yellow can create a feeling of harmony, but in bright shades it can make some people uneasy.

Now, whether use of color will make dull employees jump up and turn handsprings is debatable, but if nothing else, a little color makes a statement that management is willing to splurge a little on the employees' creature comforts.

So how do you add color to your office? You can provide color with artwork, or you can paint your walls in creative ways. This color need not be everywhere. In fact, painting three walls off-white and one wall with a strong accent color can be more effective than surrounding people with intense color. Your choices of carpet and fabric upholstery also influence the color tones of the workspace.

Finally, if you don't want to break out the paint cans and brushes, you can always buy a few plants or artificial flowers and sprinkle them around the place at little expense.

LET THERE BE LIGHT!

Light also influences how people perceive color. Fluorescent light amplifies cooler colors such as blues, but drains warmer colors such as red; that's why fluorescent light makes most humans look awful—it drains the pinks and oranges from our flesh color. Daylight or incandescent light works the opposite way: Cooler colors pale, while warmer colors become more vibrant.

In addition, light affects how people feel about their workspace. You may have heard about a condition called seasonal affective disorder (SAD), which causes depression in susceptible people who are negatively affected by the lack of bright light during the winter months. Likewise, a perpetually dark workplace can cause depression in some employees and can result in lethargy and despondency in others. In short, lighten up if you want to motivate your work force!

TIP

If cramped working quarters are a problem, use low-intensity colors. *Intensity* refers to the saturation of the color; for example, in the red hue, pink has less intensity than deep red. High-intensity colors make a room seem smaller. Darker shades of colors also make rooms seem smaller because they absorb light.

MUSIC, MUSIC, MUSIC!

Playing music in the workplace is a tricky thing. Music distracts some people, while others find that their productivity increases when set to a beat. If you decide to allow your workers to play music in the office, make sure that everyone is in agreement about the policy. If not, you'll have to ensure that those who *do* play music in their personal workspaces do so at a volume that doesn't carry to those nearby. Naughty lyrics could also push the sexual harassment envelope, so make sure that everyone understands the limits of personal taste.

Needless to say, music isn't a universal panacea. If you decide that background music throughout the workplace during the day is impractical, you might be able to compromise. For example, each week you could take a poll to find out what style of music your employees would like to hear and then pipe it in between 4:00 and 5:00 every Friday afternoon. This approach can work for several reasons, including these:

- Most people are ready to break out of the working mode on Friday afternoon.

- It's often dress-down day, so it fits the mood.

- Rarely are clients or visitors in an office at the end of the day on Friday.

- Playing upbeat music can leave employees feeling good about their jobs when they leave for the weekend, even if they've had a terrible week.

- Allowing employees to vote on the weekly selection gives them a sense of involvement and community.

- If somebody finds it hard to work with music playing, you've picked one of the lowest productivity hours of the week to affect him or her, so the damage will be minimal. Just reassure that person that not producing much during that time is not a problem, and thank him or her for being patient.

TIP

Don't have a CD player at work? Tune a radio to the local station that plays the kind of music you want that week. Yes, commercials are a bit annoying, but even they make for a refreshing change of pace.

Here's another extension of the music idea: If you throw an off-site Christmas party with live entertainment, consider taping the band (with its permission, of course). Then replay the tape on a Friday in August to remind employees of the fun they had the year before.

ERGONOMICS MEANS SAFE AND COMFORTABLE

Ergonomics has been a buzzword in business for many years now. Simply put, ergonomics is the study of how working conditions affect our bodies. Ergonomics in a factory setting relates not only to worker comfort, but often to employee safety as well. The addition of word processing and computing as almost constant activities for many workers has kept associated strains and ergonomics in the forefront of management thinking.

Providing a workplace with comfortable and safe physical conditions increases productivity and decreases absenteeism and workman's compensation claims. It also can make your employees feel that management cares about their health and safety, which is a big morale booster.

PLAIN ENGLISH

Ergonomics is the design and use of furniture and other tools to reduce physical strain on employees.

If you work at a large company, it's likely that your facilities department purchased chairs and other equipment that meet Occupational Safety & Health Administration (OSHA) requirements. However, there are some other tools and furnishings worth installing to help people feel more comfortable.

ERGONOMIC PERKS: HEADSETS, FOOTRESTS, AND MORE

If you work at a large company, it's likely that many things about your office setup will be generic and out of your control. But if you're the owner or manager, you usually have discretion over smaller purchases. If so, consider some of these items. Most of them cost $50 or less, but they will make work much easier on the body:

- A footrest, to ease lower back strain

- A headset, for those who spend hours on the phone

- A lumbar support cushion (a desk chair pillow that supports the lower back)

- A copy holder (whether stand-alone or mounted to the computer monitor), to reduce eyestrain

TIP

Here's something that will help your workers without costing you a dime: Recommend that they make a habit of moving about during the day. Getting up from their chairs, moving their eyes away from the computer screen, and adjusting their chair height now and then helps keep them from straining their bodies and from becoming stiff and inflexible.

COMPUTERS AND PRODUCTIVITY

One of the most talked-about ergonomic hot spots today is the computing station. The repetitive nature of many computing tasks, such as typing and clicking the mouse, can cause serious injury. Eyestrain is also a concern when a worker stares at light rays emanating from a screen most of the day.

You can implement many things to ease strain and keep workers happy while they compute. Here are just a few:

- A wrist rest

- An ergonomic keyboard

- A trackball mouse

- A touchpad

- A glare-reduction screen

- An under-the-desk keyboard drawer

 TIP

If an employee suffers from carpal tunnel syndrome as a result of repetitive keyboarding, consider voice recognition software. Although its functionality is still a little clumsy, this technology allows those unable to use computers because of injury or lack of skill to enter text by speaking into a headset microphone.

THE 30-SECOND RECAP

- Although getting rid of demotivators won't in itself motivate people, it can improve the morale of employees.

- Color and light can be used to subconsciously motivate productivity or to give a sense of space to employees.

- Musical interludes might be the perfect way to break up or end the work week.

- The right furniture and accessories can make repetitive work easier to handle and can keep employees more productive and healthy.

Lesson 4

Giving Them What They Need to Succeed

In this lesson, you get some ideas about motivating your people by providing them with what they need to be successful.

Imagine this: You're on top of a ladder, you've got a mouthful of nails, you're juggling a stack of pictures to hang, and you realize that you left the hammer on the kitchen counter. That's kind of what it feels like when you've got work to do at the office and you don't have the proper tools.

One of the most demotivating things in the world is not having the knowledge or equipment to do what you have to do. This chapter looks at some of the things you can give workers to help them succeed.

Training the Troops: From On-the-Job Training to a Degree

You hire people because they have certain qualifications. These qualifications might include a college degree or specific work experience, such as experience with certain software programs or pieces of equipment.

But nobody comes equipped with everything he or she needs to work at your specific company, with all its homegrown procedures and processes. And it's human nature to want to continually evolve and learn new things. So, from the day you start working with an

employee, that person will look to you for training to help her succeed
and move forward in her career.

TIP

> Try asking job candidates what training they would
> like when you interview them. Their answers can tell
> you whether they understand what skills are
> required for this position. You'll also learn whether
> they are forward thinking about their future with
> your company.

THE RIGHT START

The first thing you owe an employee is the right training, starting
on his first day at your company. Many people begin training an
employee by lecturing him about company policies and procedures.
Often, though, it's more efficient to ask a few questions first. Here are
a few to get you started:

- Ask what the employee already knows about the company,
  his job, and the road ahead. Why waste time teaching what
  he has already learned?

- Ask how he learns best. Some people like to be shown; others like to try themselves. Some like to take all the manuals
  and guidelines for their job and lock themselves away in a
  cubicle for three days; others like to just walk around and
  observe for a while.

- Ask what processes he already understands but needs more
  practice to master.

- Ask how he did his job at his last place of employment. Not
  only might you get a few tips about how to improve your
  own processes, but you'll also figure out what the employee
  might have to unlearn to fit in with your crew.

After you have the answers to these questions, you can begin to train. Here are general techniques I recommend for effective training:

- Hold a meeting to go over the main responsibilities of the job, from manager to employee. During this discussion, provide a description of the main job responsibilities, give an overview of the processes involved, and be very clear about your expectations, both in general and as they apply to this employee.

- Assign a *mentor* to work with the new employee on a day-to-day basis. Have the new employee work alongside the mentor for a few days or a week, observing and taking notes.

- After the employee has observed the work for a few days, sit down again and go over everything you went over in your first discussion. You must repeat this information because you can't expect an employee to have grasped even 20 percent of what you talked about the first day—everything was too new to have stuck. However, by observing the job for a few days, the employee should now be able to absorb what you have to say and to ask intelligent questions.

- Assign some specific process, and have the mentor observe the employee as she performs it. Give her constructive feedback on her performance. If all goes well, the employee should be able to try that process on her own, but she should always feel free to come back to you or her mentor with questions.

PLAIN ENGLISH

A **mentor** is a trusted counselor or guide. Mentors impart knowledge to others based on their real-world experience.

CAUTION

If you're using mentoring in the workplace, be sure that you support those mentors. As their manager, you have to allow them the time they need to help others in addition to doing their own work. Mentoring can be rewarding if people are given what they need to do it right.

Of course, different jobs require different amounts and types of training. In general, though, following the pattern outlined here (giving an overview, allowing the employee to observe the work, providing another overview, and letting the employee try the process under supervision) helps most people get off to a good start.

CAUTION

Be sure to let a new employee know that you don't expect him to absorb all you're telling him on the first day. By telling him that you'll go over it all again, you take some of the pressure off and allow him to really listen to what you're saying.

Learning on the Job

Don't make the mistake of thinking that learning stops once an employee masters his or her job. In fact, being able to pick up new skills on a regular basis is an important motivator that keeps people doing the same job at the same company for many years to come.

TIP

Always emphasize to employees that you welcome their questions and concerns. Many people don't learn new skills because they're afraid to ask questions.

You can structure ongoing learning into every job by using a few simple techniques. First, remember that doing one's job well often requires an understanding of other areas of the business. Allow your employees to interact with and observe other departments'—or even other vendors'—operations. By doing so, your employees will better understand what impact their work has on others. In addition, this exposure shows them options for their future growth in the company, which could lie in another department or type of work.

Second, practice stretching your employees' abilities. If they perform some tasks well, put them in situations in which they can excel. If they have supervised a small group of people on a project well, for instance, up the ante and have them supervise a larger group. If they successfully organized a meeting for 30 people, have them plan and coordinate a trade show. Even though these tasks might not be part of their regular job, try adding a few things to their responsibilities now and then to see whether they can handle them. People always learn in new situations.

Third, expose your employees to other people who might know techniques they don't. You started that on day one with a mentoring scenario. Remember that the appropriate mentor for an employee might change as time goes by; the person who knew more than the employee on the first day might not be the right mentor a year from now. Have other managers share their skills and experience with the people in your department. Observing people who are really knowledgeable in action is a great education.

TIP

Don't be so egotistical that you're afraid to admit your own weaknesses. If another manager at the company knows more about some area of your business or has a strength in an area you don't, swallow your pride and ask that person to share the knowledge with you and your staff.

Finally, make sure that you dedicate part of every performance review to a discussion of training. If an area of the employee's performance is weak, consider recommending that the person receive additional mentoring or take a class or seminar.

LEARNING ONLINE

Many companies today employ whole training departments that see to employees' classroom learning experiences. Many companies offer classes ranging from how to use a software product to negotiating skills, and from business ethics to sexual harassment policies. Sometimes on-staff trainers teach; other times, people attend an off-site training facility for a day or two.

TIP

> When you get catalogs in the mail from training companies, don't toss them; save them in a folder. Then place the folder where all your employees have access to it so that they can get ideas for the training programs they would like to see the company offer.

Your employees might benefit from additional educational opportunities as well. Online training is an option that offers great convenience in these busy times. Also called *distance learning,* online training allows employees to take a course over the Internet from home, from their desks, or even from the road.

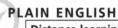

PLAIN ENGLISH

> **Distance learning** is any structured learning that takes advantage of communication media, such as computers and videotapes, to allow learners to study in a remote location but under the guidance of an instructor or educational institution.

Online training opportunities range from those that allow people to download and print information and submit tests by e-mail to live interaction between a remote trainer and student online. Many companies also run video-conferences to train people in the field. Regardless of whether your company is willing to invest in certain technologies to enable distance learning or whether you simply encourage your employees to look for online courses they would like to take on their own time, this form of training is definitely the wave of the future.

Tuition Reimbursement

Today most companies offer some form of tuition reimbursement. Under this kind of program, the company reimburses an employee for all or some of the costs of tuition and textbooks. Reimbursement can be as informal as a manager okaying attendance at a one-day seminar on Windows to a formal program that helps employees get a college degree.

Tuition reimbursement is usually tied into two key factors: First, the coursework must be logically related to the employee's work responsibilities. Second, the employee must obtain an acceptable grade in the class.

Learn your company's tuition reimbursement policy, and make that information available to your employees. Make sure they know what they need to do to be eligible and how much reimbursement they can expect. Tuition programs are great perks that make employees more valuable to you and that help them get ahead in their careers. Unfortunately, people often don't take advantage of these programs just because they're in the dark about what's involved.

Providing the Proper Tools

Training gives people the knowledge they need to do their job. But it's important that you also ensure that your employees have other things to help them succeed. These include a little peace and quiet and the right technology.

A LITTLE PRIVACY, PLEASE!

Some jobs require constant interaction. Others require complete concentration and quiet. But everybody needs a little peace now and then. Often you can't do much about the office setup and how private or public workstations are, but you can be sensitive to the need for getting away now and then. Try a few of these strategies to give your people some needed quiet time during the day:

- Allow flex time so that people can come in and leave early, or come in and stay late to get work done when it's quieter.

- Make an office available to people who have a project they need to concentrate on. If nothing else, make your office available on a rotating basis when you're at lunch or at a meeting.

- Allow people to work at home when they have to meet a tough deadline.

- Establish a quiet time one afternoon a week when people are not to disturb each other, unless it's a dire emergency.

TIP

> One company I worked for gave out plastic disks that were green on one side and red on the other. If someone didn't want to be disturbed, he or she hung the red disk on the door or cubicle. If the green side of the disk was turned out, it was okay to talk to that person. This approach gave employees some control over their own privacy.

THE OFFICE MAMBO

Of course, the ultimate in private work space is an office of one's own. For many people, an office is like the Holy Grail of corporate America. The bigger the office, the more windows—and the better the view—the more successful they feel. Needless to say, there is both a practical gain of simply having more privacy and space to get work done and the psychological benefit that comes from having a bigger and better work space. It's a sign of status and success.

Even if you don't care what kind of space *you* work in, don't forget how your employees feel about their work space. Watch for opportunities to reward good performance with better accommodations. Moving from a cubicle into an office can work wonders in the motivation department. Moving from a small office to a bigger one can do almost as much.

CAUTION

At all costs, try to avoid giving someone a quality of work space that you have to take away at a later date. If you give someone a window office once, he or she will be totally demotivated if the window is lost when the company reorganizes or makes an office move.

PENS, PAPER, A 500MHZ PENTIUM?

If you think about it, you'll decide that a large part of being a manager or supervisor is being a glorified office supply sergeant. Even if handing somebody a $5 calculator might not seem particularly motivating, it certainly is if the employee needs it to perform his or her job. Indeed, management sends a very negative message if it does not provide its employees with the tools they need to succeed. You might not be able to procure state-of-the-art computers for everyone in your group, but you should make it part of your job to listen carefully to what people need and then to do your best to provide it.

Here is a checklist of items that might make your employees' work lives a little easier to manage:

- Current versions of software, such as Microsoft Office and Windows or Corel WordPerfect

- Additional memory or upgraded motherboards for computers

- Modems that allow faster access to the Internet

- A personal information manager, such as the Palm Pilot

- Contact-management software for busy salespeople or customer service folks

- A pager or cell phone to help people stay in touch if they're on the road a great deal

- Basic supplies such as a calendar or organizer, a Rolodex, and a phone with features they need, such as mute or conference

- Ergonomic items, such as a wrist rest and a foot rest

TIP

If you can't get the go-ahead from management to purchase what an employee needs, consider sharing an item, such as a department laptop computer, among all employees. If nothing else, acknowledge that you appreciate the fact that it's challenging for an employee to work without the item.

THE 30-SECOND RECAP

- People need good training as they begin a job, in addition to ongoing learning opportunities.

- Training can occur in a class, on the job, or online.

- Online training can save time and be more convenient than attending classes in person.

- Work space can provide privacy, quiet for concentration, and status to motivate employees.

- Give people the tools they need to do their work successfully, from basic office supplies to high-tech equipment.

LESSON 5
Go Team!

In this lesson, you learn the importance of team spirit in motivating employees.

This chapter concerns one of the most overused motivational strategies in business today: team building. So many people are talking the talk of team building without really building a team-oriented workplace that it has left employees somewhat dubious. How can you breathe fresh life into a technique that many employees have come to discount and even dread?

First, you have to remember that the basic concept of teamwork, fueled by the driving force of leadership, is a sound one. You simply have to understand how to make teamwork become more than just a label among your workgroup. Once you really understand how team building works, you can use some of the suggestions in this chapter to give this motivator a shot in the arm at your company.

TEAMWORK TODAY

Although it seems as though the concept of team building has been lurking around the corporate hallways in the form of buzzwords and workshops for a long time now, it's a relatively recent addition. To a large extent, the workplace of 50 years ago was based on a vertical hierarchy in which rigid job descriptions defined one's contribution to the whole.

As society became more prosperous, workers became better educated, our economy offered more choices, and people began to question these rigid roles. Studies on team building began in the late 1940s but really took off in the 1950s, when programs that assisted veterans in obtaining an education became widespread and there was less unemployment. People began to look to the workplace to do more than just provide a paycheck. In this more democratic working climate, team-building theories began to proliferate.

These theories aimed to motivate employees with several strategies and desired outcomes. Team building is supposed to accomplish these goals:

- Make employees feel that their contributions are valued.

- Acknowledge that no goal is reached without the contribution of everybody working toward it, no matter what their positions are in the hierarchy.

- Generate loyalty by making employees feel that their *team* (company) is somehow better than others are.

- Encourage respect and trust among team members.

- Enable more effective communication.

PLAIN ENGLISH

Teams are groups of people with a common goal who use the unique strengths of each member and the combined strengths of the group to achieve that goal.

But today, team building is often a mandate handed down in a company memo to managers rather than a long-term commitment to sound team-building practices. Managers aren't trained in sound leadership and team-building practices (unless you consider a one-day workshop every few years to be training). The result is that a few managers with innate leadership abilities have made team building work, while the majority of managers have stumbled around spouting bad sports analogies.

WHAT MAKES A GOOD TEAM?

Not all teams are created equal, although some team-building theories treat them as if they were. A brand new team has different opportunities and challenges than an existing team riddled with conflicts and politics. Likewise, large teams are different than small teams. *Decision teams*, such as an executive committee that votes on policy decisions, have different mandates than *work teams*, which work together on day-to-day tasks to reach measurable goals.

PLAIN ENGLISH

Decision teams function primarily to make decisions. An example would be a committee formed to review flex time policies at a company. **Work teams** have to coordinate individual efforts on a day-to-day basis to perform tasks; a space shuttle crew is a work team.

But although teams may differ, successful teams are built on some basic precepts:

- **Trust.** Building a sense of trust among team members is vital to an open team structure.

- **Communication.** Opening up avenues of communication among members ensures that everybody understands the goals of the larger group and knows how his or her individual work fits in.

- **Involvement.** One key to creating a successful team is to obtain the commitment of all team members to key decisions. This doesn't necessarily mean that everything gets done by consensus, but each member should be aware of the decisions and should understand why they are made.

- **Conflict resolution.** Within good teams, conflict is brought into the open and is resolved as quickly as possible.

- **Feedback.** In a successful team, the manager or other team members provide feedback on a regular basis so that all members can work together to improve the team's performance.

CAUTION

One basic principle of team building has been expressed this way: Team building is a process, not an event. Don't expect to implement team building in a day!

WHEN DOES A GROUP BECOME A TEAM?

Every team has a leader, and more will be said about the quality of leadership later in this chapter. But how else does a group of people differ from a team of people? Compare the qualities on this chart to understand this key difference.

Groups	Teams
No formal communications procedures	Communication procedures in place
No support for each others' activities	Support for each others' activities
No overriding vision	Vision and goals provided by the leader or by consensus
Subgroups formed randomly	Focus on working together as a single group
No group identity	Self-esteem formed through group identity
Individual contributions not encouraged	Individual contributions welcomed

A group does not automatically make a team. It takes some work on your part to ensure that you institute the characteristics of a team in any collection of people you work with. One of the most important vehicles for this is communication.

COMMUNICATION IS THE FOUNDATION

Communication is another buzzword in the business world. But cliché or not, good communication is the very foundation of good teams. In teams, communication serves several purposes, including these:

- **Common goals.** You must ensure that the team is in agreement about the goals and work to be performed.

- **Conflict resolution.** Make sure that conflicts are aired and resolved.

- **Problem resolution.** Catching procedural or task problems before they get out of hand.

- **Synergy.** Create a synergy of talents by using methods such as brainstorming to generate ideas and solutions that an individual alone might not be able to produce.

Good communication consists of a basic model. First, communication is initiated; for example, you send a memo to an employee. The employee receives the message, with varying amounts of noise getting in the way of understanding it. This noise can consist of things such as personal preconceptions, lack of context, or semantic interference. Finally, a response to the communication is generated, perhaps in the form of another memo or phone call.

TIP

> You can reduce the chances of miscommunication by encouraging team members to repeat or paraphrase important information you present to them.

To create successful communication, you have to encourage a communications network—that is, a series of two-way communications that ensure the information perceived is the information that was intended. That requires a sense of openness and trust among team members, one that allows them to admit confusion or to ask for clarification. As you set up communications vehicles such as weekly staff meetings, regular reports, or online chatting areas, consider the underlying need for trust and openness in your communications model.

DOES YOUR TEAM COME WITH BAGGAGE?

Now that you have an understanding of some of the characteristics of team building, how do you begin to use it on the job? One place to start is by understanding what has been done in the past to build team spirit at your workplace and how your employees feel about those efforts. Start with a little simple research:

- Talk to your Human Resources department manager to find out what efforts have been made along these lines in the past. How did these efforts go over? Did the company get employee feedback on them?

- Talk to your employees, and ask them what teamwork means to them.

- Assess whether you see the earmarks of teamwork among your group. It's easier to build on a few characteristics of teamwork that are already in place than to start from scratch.

Specifically, ask your employees these questions:

- What stops our group from being an effective team?

- How could we become a better team?

- What are we doing now that is team-oriented, and how can we build on that?

Is "Team" a Dirty Word?

I once encountered a company that had grown rapidly from a small entrepreneurial group to a large public company, yet it clung desperately to the vestiges of its younger self. As the company became too large for the whole group to fit into a single conference room, management hired professional consultants to come in and run what they called Team-Building Days.

Team-Building Days consisted of scavenger hunts and other games in which group effort counts. People were forced to wear hats that had silly team names on them, such as "Cougars" and "Pythons." They were given assignments to think of clever solutions to stupid problems. Childish prizes such as yo-yos and water pistols were distributed throughout the day. If anyone missed Team-Building Day because he was trying to make a work deadline, he was severely reprimanded.

How did the employees feel about this enforced team building? They hated it. They could see, better than senior management could, that the young company was feeling growing pains and the loss of its entrepreneurial childhood, and was trying desperately to live in the past. But searching for your entrepreneurial roots isn't team building—and a once-a-year fun-fest doesn't build trust or lay the foundations for teamwork.

TIP

A whole subset of people resent teamwork not because of its concepts, but because of its language. Analyze your own speech for clichés and tired sports analogies (like comparing the last part of a project to the homestretch or final inning), and get rid of them!

The point is that teamwork is not something you can drag out a few times a year, and it's not something you can jam down people's throats. If you implement team-building practices on a daily basis and work with your employees to make sure they buy in, you will find a team environment to be a powerful motivator.

MAKE IT LAST

After you've polled your employees for their attitudes about teams, you need to assess the commitment of senior management to the concept. In 1994, one survey found that although most companies spouted team building as a policy, only 22 percent actually had any kind of team-building program in place. Here are the most common reasons companies gave for not using team-building programs:

- Managers didn't know how to build teams.

- Managers didn't understand the payoff of spending time on team building.

- Team-building efforts weren't rewarded in the company.

- People felt that their teams were doing okay; they didn't need team building.

- People felt that management didn't support team building.

Note the second, fourth, and fifth items. Each of these suggests that a manager runs the risk of employees questioning team-building efforts in an organization in which team building isn't supported from the top.

Can you instill more team-oriented activity in your workgroup without broader support? Yes. By doing so, you might make productive changes in employee motivation and attitude. But, as with any motivational effort, the time a manager or supervisor spends on team-building is ultimately going to be supported or questioned by your management. Seeking support early on will not only make your task easier, it will also show employees that the team-building talk isn't only one layer of management deep.

TIP

> You can find one big clue as to how teamwork is viewed at your company in your company mission statement (it's there in a memo at the bottom of your drawer or in the back of the employee handbook). See if teamwork is part of the greater mandate for your organization. If it isn't, suggest that it should be.

When you understand how management feels about team building and have gathered your employees' attitudes about it, start to work the basic elements of team building (trust, communication, involvement, conflict resolution, and feedback) into your workplace. Don't announce it at the staff meeting as a great new program. Do start to practice it on a daily basis!

LEADERSHIP: IT'S ESSENTIAL TO A SUCCESSFUL TEAM

Now this is the difficult part. Putting the precepts of teamwork up on a bulletin board doesn't make a team. The hard truth is that, to a great extent, a team is formed by the leadership it receives. Thus, the most serious work you can do to establish a team environment is to work on your leadership skills.

Some people are born leaders, and others have leadership thrust upon them. Regardless, you can cultivate certain characteristics of leadership.

INNOVATION IS KEY

Consider the words *manager* and *leader* for a moment. Here are definitions that might help:

- A manager is someone who maintains things. A manager is an administrator of processes, policies, and people.

- A leader is someone who has a vision and communicates it. A leader focuses on the long-term goal, not the day-to-day processes.

In short, a manager manages the present situation, and a leader leads the way into the future. A key part of that leadership is the willingness to innovate. Where a manager is a champion of the status quo, a leader asks questions and pokes at current policy and procedure to see if something better can be found. To a great extent, it's that willingness to be open to excellence and change, and to involve the team in those efforts, that motivates a team.

In the 1970s, a team of researchers named Berlew and Burns talked about some key characteristics of leaders. A leader, they said, carries out the following actions:

- Establishes shared values among team members

- Instills confidence in followers

- Creates organizational excitement

- Isn't afraid of introducing major change

- Empowers followers

- Gives meaning and purpose to an organization

KNOW YOUR TEAM'S STRENGTHS

One other thing will help you become a good leader: Get to know your team. Quite often managers or supervisors get into the rut of seeing their workers according to their job descriptions. But each person on your team is complex; each has strengths and weaknesses. It's your job to really understand the best way to use the whole person to get the job done.

Now I'm finally going to resort to a sports analogy. Leadership is very much akin to the role a coach plays on a sports team. A good coach knows his or her players and watches carefully throughout the game to put each player in a role that will maximize that person's usefulness. Ask yourself these questions to see where your coaching skills could use improvement:

- Do I fully understand the strengths and weaknesses of each team member?

- Am I constantly aware of whether each team member is being challenged in his or her work?

- Have I created an environment in which each worker is willing to play the role that best ensures the success of the team? Am I willing to make shifts in assignments to utilize each person in the best way?

- Do I look for opportunities to help team members grow in their areas of weakness? Even if someone will never be the star hitter, that person still has to know how to hit now and then.

OFFICE TEAM BUILDING

Even though team building cannot be a once-a-year event, it's still possible to have some fun with your teams. If you've laid the foundation for a true organizational team structure, applying it to the dynamics of your group outside of day-to-day work can be a logical extension.

CAUTION

Don't insist upon participation in team activities outside the office. If several team members participate, that will be fine. The key is not to make this out-of-the-office team effort feel forced or allow it to become a burden to those who are too busy or not inclined to join.

SPONSOR A SPORTS TEAM

Cliché sports analogies aside, sports provide a model of teamwork that cannot be denied. The trust and communication players must have to maintain their focus and get a football from one end of a field to another, for example, provide a wonderful model for your office team. Allowing your employees to spend time outside the workplace building that kind of trust can have direct benefits back on the job.

Many offices sponsor sports teams to play other companies, or they have one department play against another. Doing so builds team spirit even among the team members who choose not to play because they root for their group to win. Ask your employees if they would enjoy such an activity—and remember, keep it fun. The last thing you need is to build cliques or personal conflicts on the playing field that spill over into your working team.

GET BEHIND A CAUSE

Less time-consuming than a sports team, but often every bit as good for team building, is a cause that employees can rally around. Consider some of these group efforts:

- Sponsor an employee who is running in a charity race.

- Sponsor a poor family or child through a local or national agency. Post letters and progress reports on the company bulletin board, where everybody can read them and feel proud.

- Participate as a group in a volunteer activity. For example, man the phones for a local public radio station pledge drive.

- Organize a food or toy drive at Christmas time.

- Organize donations of food or clothing for a disaster relief effort.

TIP

> The key to making support of a cause a team-building effort is to make sure that everybody is kept apprised of the contributions to date and the impact your efforts are having. Announce progress in the team meeting every week to keep people interested and involved.

TEAM PARAPHERNALIA

One other way to build team spirit is to engender a feeling of pride in your organization or department. You can do this by building brand loyalty, a tactic companies and sports teams have discovered with a vengeance in recent years. How is this done? Simply give people something they can wear, carry around, or display proudly on their desks that sports your company or team name or logo. In other words, give them *tchotchkes*.

PLAIN ENGLISH

> **Tchotchke,** a Yiddish word, has become a catchall phrase for small gifts or giveaways—such as note-pads, pens, or key chains—that companies give to employees or customers.

Now, these things aren't free, but their ability to provide an ongoing reminder of your team is usually worth it. If employees wear or carry the items outside the office, it's also a nice form of free advertising.

Try to find interesting items; coffee mugs, caps, and T-shirts are old standbys, but get creative!

- Mouse pads
- A customized screen saver
- Cookies with your logo baked in

- Puzzle cubes

- Water bottles

TIP

> Get together with your marketing department. These giveaway professionals might just be producing several hundred of some giveaway item for a trade show or for customers. If you can piggyback your order with theirs, that lowers the unit price for everybody.

Whatever you decide might make a nice gift, remember to make it a reminder of the intangible things you're doing to provide leadership and an environment where true team spirit can thrive.

THE 30-SECOND RECAP

- Team building must be part of your everyday work environment and cannot be a short-term effort.

- Support for team building from management is important for long-term success.

- Keystones of good teams are trust, communication, involvement, conflict resolution, and feedback.

- Good leaders provide innovation and understand how to use the skills of the team to best advantage.

- Team building can be supported by out-of-work team efforts, such as a sports team or charity efforts.

Lesson 6
Throw a Party!

In this lesson, you get some ideas for throwing successful office parties that involve and stimulate your workers.

Office parties are as inevitable as the seasons. When they go well, they're great motivators. They help people get to know each other, have a little fun, and feel relaxed with each other when they return to work. When they don't go well, they're about as pleasant as an IRS audit.

When was the last time you sat around a conference table staring at your co-workers while munching on stale cookies, trying to think of something to say? In this chapter, you'll get some insight into the role of office parties, learn some of the do's and don'ts of office parties, and discover some great ideas for how to spice them up.

The Workplace: More Than Work

Whether it's an emotionally healthy trend is debatable, but today many people depend on their offices for providing a hefty percentage of their interpersonal relationships. Many single people find that the office is the place they're most likely to meet a potential mate or form a new relationship. Even those already involved in a romantic relationship have trouble finding room in their schedules of childcare, house maintenance, and errands to socialize outside of work.

Let's face it: You spend 40 or more hours a week with these people. Not counting sleep time, you probably spend more time with co-workers than you do with your spouse or children. Few people have the luxury of having a full-time stay-at-home mate to organize their social life. So, the *socialization needs* in today's office have taken on an importance they didn't have in years past.

PLAIN ENGLISH

> **Socialization needs** comprise one of the stages of
> Abraham Maslow's hierarchy of needs; they involve
> personal fulfillment from social interaction (see
> Chapter 1, "What Motivates People?").

This is not to suggest that you have to become a social director. Work
is work, and companies that waste too much time throwing little parties or organizing team games usually end up forcing people to put in
overtime to get their real work done. But because occasional parties
are part of your working reality, you might as well use them effectively to entertain and motivate your employees.

THE DYNAMICS OF SOCIALIZATION

One of the reasons we sometimes end up with dull, uncomfortable
office get-togethers is that we fail to remember that people have different personalities and different social styles. In effect, we are forcing
people to sit in a room together and have fun. When we organize an
office party, we're often putting people who are party animals in a
room with those who think that an office is strictly for work. The outcome can be unpredictable.

Outside of work, people usually choose the time and place for socializing, as well as the people to socialize with. So, in essence, you're
creating something of an artificial social scenario when you throw an
office party.

With that in mind, consider applying some of these guidelines when
you organize your next office event:

- Get as many people as possible involved in organizing the
  party so that each has a vested interest in its success.

- Plan a few topics of conversation or activities, or create a
  theme that will offer common ground to people with different
  personalities.

- Don't let the party go on forever. Aim to please the person with the lowest tolerance for socializing, and let people know it's okay to wander off even if the party is still in full swing at that time.

- If you can break up the usual office cliques so that people chat with new people, great. But people form their alliances for a reason, and if they choose to talk only to those people they talk to every day, so be it.

- Be prepared to be a facilitator. Have a few anecdotes on hand to tell to fill in the quiet moments. If you begin by sharing a personal story that's interesting or humorous, others will often be made to feel more relaxed and will chime in with their own stories.

- Don't overdo the party thing. Instead of giving a birthday party for every employee, for example, give a party every month for everybody with a birthday in that month.

 TIP

> Stuck for snappy material? Use the Internet. These days, stories, jokes, and anecdotes whiz around the World Wide Web like good wishes at a wedding. Borrow a few to relate at your next party.

HELPING PEOPLE OUT OF THEIR SHELLS

For people who love to socialize, parties will always be fun, and these people will be motivated to enjoy your workplace all the more because of them. But what do you do to make parties motivating to those who are less sociable? These work-oriented people often live to be efficient. Why not harness that efficiency to help organize the event? If these people set up the party themselves, they'll feel like it's their responsibility to make sure things go well. And remember, these people enjoy responsibility, so in their own way, they'll enjoy the party.

Make most parties optional for people who get less out of these events. Some parties will be required, but let these folks bow out of those that aren't. Even when their attendance is required, make sure they understand that they don't have to put in more than a token appearance.

AVOIDING OFFICE PARTY PITFALLS

Of course, there are some potential challenges to partying at work. You have to be concerned about the use of alcohol in the workplace, as well as the potential for sexual harassment and other inappropriate behavior that could develop.

The Department of Labor's Working Partners for an Alcohol- and Drug-Free Workplace has put together nine tips for office celebrations. They're worth repeating here:

1. **Honesty is the best policy.** Make sure your employees know your workplace substance abuse policy and that the policy addresses the use of alcoholic beverages in any work-related situations and office social functions.

2. **Post the policy.** Use every communications vehicle to make sure your employees know the policy. Prior to an office party, use breakroom bulletin boards, office e-mail, and paycheck envelopes to communicate your policy and concerns.

3. **Reinvent the office party concept.** Why have the typical office party? Try something new—an indoor carnival, a group outing to an amusement park, or a volunteer activity with a local charity.

4. **Make sure employees know when to say when.** If you do serve alcohol at an office event, make sure all employees know that they are welcome to attend and have a good time, but that they are expected to act responsibly.

5. **Make it the office party of choice.** Make sure there are plenty of alternative, nonalcoholic beverages available.

6. **Eat and be merry!** Avoid serving lots of salty, greasy, or sweet foods that tend to make people thirsty. Serve foods rich in starch and protein, which stay in the stomach longer and slow the absorption of alcohol in the bloodstream.

7. **Designate party managers.** Remind managers that even at the office party, they have responsibilities for implementing the company's alcohol and substance abuse policy.

8. **Alternative transportation.** Anticipate the need for alternative transportation for all partygoers, and make special transportation arrangements in advance of the party. Encourage all employees to make use of the alternative transportation if they have any alcohol.

9. **None for the road.** Before the party officially ends, stop serving alcohol and remove all alcoholic beverages.

CAUTION

If you do make alcohol available at your office party, check out your state laws regarding their use and your legal responsibilities.

PARTIES THAT MOTIVATE

Okay, you've looked at your party plans and whittled down the number of events you'll have in any given year. You've considered people's attitudes toward parties and thought about how to involve people in organizing events. You've learned some do's and don'ts about alcohol and behavior at parties. Now it's time for the fun stuff. Let's get into some great ideas for partying!

TIP

> If you're organizing a really big affair, consider using a consulting company that specializes in organizing themed office parties. Search for one on the Internet using keywords such as "office parties" and "corporate events."

TAKE YOUR PARTY ON THE ROAD

One obvious way to spice up your parties is to take them out of the office. Here are some company parties I've been witness to that were extra special:

- One company rented an entire amusement park for a day to celebrate its 10th anniversary.

- Another company rented a large picnic area in a African-themed wildlife park. Employees picnicked near a lake, received glasses and Frisbees with the company logo, and then were given passes to wander around and ride the elephants and pet the llamas.

- While I was working in northern California, one of my bosses took the whole gang to a nearby cheese factory for a lunch-time picnic (wine optional).

- A company I worked for in Boston rented a creepy Gothic-looking building on a university campus for a blow-out Halloween party with employees, vendors, and customers in attendance.

Avoid the hotel meeting room or corporate meeting facility if you can. Take people someplace where there's something to do, whether it's a museum, an arts performance, a zoo, or a cooking class. These employees are used to doing things together, so bring those team-oriented skills into play and get them doing, not just talking.

CAUTION

Although many options, such as zoos or museums, are fun, avoid forcing your employees to perform childish or embarrassing activities, such as flinging water balloons at each other. Unless your group is a pretty homogenous party crowd, these activities are likely to fall flat.

Focus on the Unusual

Finding a unique place to hold a party is one approach. Another is to set a fun *theme*, which can work both in and out of the office. You remember this from your high school prom, when you and your classmates chose "Paris Night," "Roaring Twenties," or "Evening in the Tropics" as your theme.

Depending on your group and the occasion, you can set a small budget with simple decorations and food, or you can go all out: Give souvenirs and prizes, and play music and games that fit the theme. The important thing is to be sensitive to your people and know whether they'll get into the spirit of a more elaborate theme party. If they won't, keep it simple.

PLAIN ENGLISH

A **theme** is a subject or topic of discourse or artistic expression. (So, get artistic with your party themes!)

Here are some thoughts that might stimulate a theme for your next office party:

- Relate the theme to work. If you're launching a new product or service, for example, see if you can use its name to spark a theme. A new product called Summit Faucets, for instance, could revolve around famous mountains (summits). Have an ice sculpture of Mt. Everest, Mt. St. Helens canapés, and Pike's Peak punch!

- A theme can involve a place (such as Paris, for the opening of your first European office, with an Eiffel Tower-shaped cake and can-can dancer finger puppets) or an event (such as the American Revolution for the introduction of a revolutionary new product line; use red, white, and blue liberally).

- Have people wear costumes if you think they will be comfortable with that. Give prizes not only for the most imaginative costume, but also for creative categories such as the cheapest costume and the most outrageous.

- Use your theme to direct conversation or play a game. If the theme is Mardi Gras, play a trivia game about celebrations around the world.

TIP

Don't limit your themes to places and events on earth. How about a Star Trek party, a sixth-dimension party, or a come-as-your-favorite-space-alien party?

TEN GREAT PARTY IDEAS

Okay, here are my 10 most creative ideas for a party. Borrow any you like:

1. Invite employees to bring their pets into the office (located in an easy-to-clean-up area such as your warehouse, in case of animal accidents). Hold a pet parade, a best pet story contest, or a pet obstacle course competition.

2. For your Christmas party, rent out a local indoor skating rink for an evening, and have the event catered.

3. To celebrate hitting a long-awaited goal, such as record sales numbers, throw a bingo party. The first one to get the record profit number on the card wins a prize!

4. Throw a funky movie party. Let employees vote on their favorite quirky movie from a list you provide, and then show the movie in your largest conference room or rent out a local movie theatre. Provide fresh popcorn, and encourage people to goof on the movie all they want.

5. Choose a campy TV show of today or yesteryear, and throw a theme party. A Monty Python party, for example, would have people holding Ministry of Funny Walk contests, dead parrot competitions, and Spanish Inquisition quiz games.

6. If everyone complains about the fattening food you usually serve, get away from the cookies and chips and throw a healthy party. Supply fresh fruit, raw veggies with low-fat dip, and diet drinks. Rent out an exercise facility as the site of the party. Let people come in sweats and use the treadmills and other equipment during the event. Make sure it's all in fun and that everybody—no matter what shape he or she is in—has something to do.

7. Have a musical party. Let people bring in musical instruments and jam, hold singing contests, and run a *Name That Tune*-like trivia game. Be sure to include a wide spectrum of musical styles so those not up on current pop music have expertise to contribute.

8. Throw a founder's year party. Figure out the year your company was founded, and have everybody come dressed in clothes of the time. This works best if your company is more than 50 years old, but even a 20-year-old company will send employees researching trends and hot news stories of the 1970s and 1980s.

9. Hold a party on the birthday for the person who invented the product you make. If you make light bulbs, throw a Thomas Edison birthday party. If you publish books, honor Guttenburg. If you're a pharmaceutical company, try Madame Curie or Jonas Salk.

10. For a smaller group, buy one of those murder mystery party kits and have everybody play a part. Or, write your own mystery revolving around a little-known new employee who is found dead of overwork in the lunchroom. Your employees' assignment: Find the manager who assigned such a deadly workload!

TIP

> If you have the choice between several low-budget small parties and one bigger one, why not go for the bigger one and go all out? The promise of the bigger event several months ahead can be just as motivating in its anticipation as parties occurring every month or so.

By putting a little more creativity and thought into office social events, you can turn them from dreaded obligations to motivational energizers!

THE 30-SECOND RECAP

- If you plan them properly, parties can be a fun and motivating experience.

- Remember that people socialize differently, and people respond differently to the essentially enforced socializing of an office party.

- Be sensitive to the people who don't enjoy social events as much as others, and find ways to make them more comfortable with office events.

- Be careful when involving alcohol in a company event, and know your company's liabilities in such a situation.

- Spice up parties by holding them out of the office at a unique location or setting them to a fun theme.

LESSON 7
Give a Gift

In this lesson, you get some ideas for gift giving that will keep your team spirit on track.

Giving gifts is an age-old custom in many cultures. In some countries, such as Japan, it's practically a science. A gift can be used to express respect, affection, gratitude, or appreciation.

Over the years, giving business gifts to motivate employees has become an accepted practice. As long as you take care to keep the gifts professionally appropriate, your gift incentives are limited only by the boundaries of your own creativity.

GIFT GIVING AS MOTIVATION

Think for a moment about Ebenezer Scrooge in the Dickens classic, *A Christmas Carol*. Remember when the Ghost of Christmas Past reminds him of the holiday parties his old employer used to throw? Scrooge grudgingly admits that even though they cost his employer only a few pounds, the happiness those parties brought the staff was immeasurable.

That's kind of how gifts work as motivators on the job. They don't have to cost a lot, but they say to employees that their management thinks of them as more than just workers. They show that the company pays attention to the employees when they go the extra mile and demonstrates that loyalty and hard work are valued.

CAUTION

Giving presents is not designed to be a substitute for providing a well-rounded work environment. Cookies get stale very quickly when salaries are low, opportunity is scarce, and policies are stifling.

THE RIGHT TIME

The appropriate occasions for giving a gift can be many and varied. A gift tied to performance or meeting a certain goal is a great incentive. A gift for no reason at all, especially when morale or energy is running a little low, often works wonders as well. Here are a few other times when giving a gift is a natural motivator:

- On each employee's birthday or working anniversary, or for everyone at holiday time.

- When a team achieves a goal or milestone on a project (and you can give just one gift for the whole group).

- Any time a customer takes the time to tell you he received great service from a particular employee.

- When someone goes outside his or her own job description to help a co-worker. This discourages the dreaded it's-not-my-job attitude.

- As a reward for a tedious or menial task well done, such as when a particular employee has ordered and picked up everyone's dinner during late-night sessions, when ordering dinner isn't part of anyone's job description.

TIP

> People don't often think of it, but having employees
> give a gift to a manager is also an occasion for fun.
> At one job, I rallied my employees to put together a
> collage of relevant paperwork and framed it as a gift
> when my manager finished negotiating a very tough
> deal to our department's benefit. It was fun for
> them and was very appreciated by our manager!

GUIDELINES FOR GIVING

Here are some general do's and don'ts for gift giving at work:

- **Use discretion.** Be very careful not to give gifts that are
  unrelated to specific work performance to one individual. Not
  only does that suggest favoritism to this employee, but it also
  can suggest a form of sexual harassment to the recipient or to
  your Human Resources Department.

- **Variety is key.** Vary the gifts you give so that they don't
  become old hat. If you sent cookies last month, spring for
  coffee mugs with the team name on them next month.

- **Don't use gifts as bribes.** Gifts are gifts—they don't come
  with strings attached. A gift should simply be your way of
  expressing appreciation.

- **Do give appropriate gifts.** Anything that's sexually sugges-
  tive or in poor taste doesn't belong in your office and could
  land you in hot water.

- **Don't overdo.** After all, this isn't a social club; it's work.
  When all is said and done, remember that an employee is
  likely to appreciate 10 minutes of your undivided attention to
  help him solve a problem more than a red rose on his desk
  every month.

- **Be creative.** Have fun with gifts: Nobody needs six coffee mugs with the company logo when, for the same money, they could get tickets for a popular concert or a roll of quarters for an afternoon at the local video arcade.

SHOPPING FOR GIFTS

Congratulations—you live in an age when you can buy anything and everything over the Internet. This use of *e-commerce* can be a tremendous saver of both time and money in the business gift-giving department. You can usually get things shipped for free, and they generally arrive within a few days of placing your order.

PLAIN ENGLISH

> **E-Commerce** is the buying or selling of anything online through the use of the Internet.

If you're not an online shopper, haunt your local mall. Check out those kiosks in the center of the mall. Some offer personalized gifts such as desk pen sets or glasses with employee initials, although these are much pricier than buying through catalogs or online. Also keep an office supply catalog handy; many include business gift items such as fancy pens or tins of caramel popcorn, and the companies usually deliver.

You might want to set a budget at the beginning of each year for gifts to your employees, and then buy some items at a discount store to save money. That way you'll have some things on hand to give at the spur of the moment.

TIP

> To find great gift ideas, try searching the World Wide Web with the keywords "business gifts," "corporate gifts," or "promotional products."

ONLINE SHOPPING

Probably hundreds of thousands of online sites have products that
your employees might enjoy.

TIP

Try to deal with more reputable sites, especially
when buying large quantities of items. Make sure
they have good customer support, a reasonable
return policy, and security for exchanging credit card
information online.

To get you started, here's a small selection of Web sites you might
want to explore for interesting business gifts:

- **Diamond Promotions, www.logomall.com.** This site features various customized business gifts such as pads, mugs,
  shirts, and so on. Check out the Promotional Idea Showcase
  for gift ideas, or read a copy of *Imprint*, a quarterly publication on promotional gift giving.

- **Just Gift Baskets, www.justgiftbaskets.com.** Here you can
  select from coffee, tea, cookies, dried fruits, and baskets with
  assorted goodies.

- **Virtual Florist, www.virtualflorist.com.** This site offers
  both flowers and free electronic cards. There's even an Office
  Chat card selection with messages such as "Take the Day
  Off" and "What a Great Idea."

- **Promotional Products, www.promotionalproductss.net.**
  This site offers a wide assortment of customized business
  gifts, such as calendars, mouse pads, and so on, on which you
  can silk-screen your logo or company name.

- **Corporate Gifts Network, at www.corp-gifts.net.** This one
  is slightly more sophisticated, with gift baskets including
  items such as wine and caviar, as well as the more typical
  fruit and cookie packages.

- **Music Gift Spot, www.musicgiftspot.com.** Want some real
  fun? How about ordering an assortment of toy musical instruments, such as musical spoons and finger cymbals for your
  next staff meeting?

TIP

If you're going to have items customized, remember
that it might take a little more time, and you'll probably have to provide artwork if you want your logo
included. Also, verify who pays for shipping before
you place your order.

GIFTS: FROM APPLES TO ZEBRAS

So, what kinds of things make good office gifts? Here are several
ideas to get you going:

- Any kind of food, including cookies, candy, pizza ordered in
  for a lunch-time or late-night meeting, fruit, and almost anything chocolate.

- Computer accessories, such as mouse pads, screen savers,
  and wrist rests.

- Desktop toys, such as stress balls or mini-Slinkys. These have
  the added benefit of helping your employees relax or even
  think a little more creatively in the middle of a mind-numbing
  day.

- Personalized notepads, each with an individual employee's
  name on top. These have the added benefit of being practical
  personalized notes employees can include with correspon-
  dence to customers or vendors.

- Unusual business card or pen holders for employees' desks.
  Rather than the standard plastic holders, how about small
  wicker baskets you can buy cheaply at discount stores?

- Cool Pez dispensers.

- Tickets to events, such as sports, movies, or concerts.

- A visit from a masseuse. Set up the masseuse in a central location, and have people sign up to get a 10-minute neck massage.

- A $5 donation in each employee's name to a charity of their choice.

- A popular CD, book, or video. Just make sure there's nothing offensive to anyone in the contents of these items.

- A visit from a magician. Invite the magician to come to the office for a day and wander around, entertaining the troops as they work.

 TIP

> Don't forget to team up with your marketing department: They often order company-specific promotional items in bulk and can tack on your order for savings. You can also let them do the work of ordering and providing logo artwork.

FREE COMPANY STUFF

When choosing gifts, don't forget about your own company's products or services. Obviously, if you make nuts and bolts, a gift box of company products is less fun than if you're a toy manufacturer handing out free toys. But think about it: You might just have something employees want.

You either can offer these products or services free of charge, or you can give employees a great discount to purchase them themselves. If your company thinks to order a certain number of extra products, you'll reduce the manufacturing costs and keep the price low for your employees.

For example, I've worked for book publishers who make all their titles available to employees. One publisher let employees order one of every title for free (we're talking about more than 300 books here), then charged them 50 percent off the cover price for additional copies. Another charged only the cost of manufacturing the book (often only a couple dollars for a $20 book). Another company I worked for owned a huge chain of video rental stores. Employees could order videos at a substantial discount. When I worked for a major national magazine, a free copy of the magazine showed up on my desk every week.

If you work for a service company, you can offer your company services to employees for free or at a discount. For example, if one of your services is carpet cleaning, offer employees a once-a-year free carpet cleaning, or perhaps an upholstery cleaning at 25 percent of the regular price.

 TIP

> After establishing good business relationships with suppliers or customers, you might be able to buy products that might appeal to your workers and then offer them at discount. For example, you might make plastic grommets for sneakers, but the company you sell them to might offer your employees sneakers at a discount.

THANKING THE FAMILY

Most employers forget the fact that most employees have a family—a family who supports the employee when he or she works long hours or is under particular stress. A wonderful and often quite unexpected gesture is to take the time to thank the family of that employee for its support. Try some of these ways to show your appreciation:

- Write a thank-you note to the employee's significant other after a bout of frequent travel or a few late nights of work.

- Send a turkey or cheesecake home with each employee at holiday time (many companies used to do this, but the tradition seems to have fallen off over time).

- Throw an open house for families, complete with refreshments and even entertainment. Invite spouses and children to visit the office during a slow period so that they can see what their father/mother/wife/husband/significant other does all day.

- Invite families to holiday parties. One company I worked for even flew in employees from remote locations, along with their spouses, for the holiday party.

- Offer to fly a spouse along on a business trip to a particularly fun spot.

Remembering to thank the family is just another way to tell your employee that you see him or her as a person, and not just a job title.

THE 30-SECOND RECAP

- Give gifts to show employees appreciation or gratitude.

- Make sure gifts are appropriate for a business setting.

- The Internet provides a great way to shop for business gifts.

- Consider whether your company's products or services might make good gifts or can be offered to employees at a discount.

- Try sending thank-you notes or gifts to an employee's family in appreciation for supporting the employee and all he or she does for the company.

Lesson 8
Getting Out of the Office

In this lesson, you learn about the benefits of getting people out of the traditional office setting.

Think about it: When you have only a week or two per year for vacation, do you sit around the same house you've been sitting around all year, or do you go somewhere else? When people want to renew or refresh themselves, many head for a change of scenery. Workers are no different—even the most attractive and pleasant workplace gets tiresome after a while. At some point, employees begin to measure the dynamics of the workplace by the number of feet they walk from their cubicle to the coffee pot, a number that never varies.

In this chapter, we'll explore some of the benefits of giving your employees a chance to work out of the office and get a new perspective on their careers.

Telecommuting: When Work Comes Home

Some call it *telecommuting*, others telework or flex work. Whatever you call it, it involves a decentralizing of your work force, allowing some of them to work part-time or even full-time from their homes.

PLAIN ENGLISH

> **Telecommuting** (also called telework or flex work) is the practice of allowing workers to work from their homes, taking advantage of various technologies to connect them to other workers and information.

According to a recent survey, more than 12 million people telecommute today, making it clear that this way of doing business is here to stay. Advances in technology and telecommunications, especially in the area of computers and the Internet, have made this lifestyle possible.

Ironically, this practice is really nothing new. In the not-so-distant Industrial Age of the late nineteenth century, workers were pulled out of their cottage-based industries into factories. That means that only a hundred years or so divides us from a time when people didn't get up, knock back a cup of coffee, and run out the door to the office. Instead, they stayed at home and made products that they sold to a company or sold directly to their community. So, telecommuting may be a lifestyle whose time has come—again!

THE BENEFITS OF TELECOMMUTING

Many debates have gone on about the pros and cons of telecommuting. But with technology providing more ease of communication and better access to centralized information, it's getting harder to argue against it.

The first thing most people consider to be a benefit of telecommuting is an increase in productivity, often cited in the 15–20 percent range. That productivity increase is thought to come from the less stressful environment found in one's own home, the lack of disturbances or downtime from casual chats in the hallway, and the removal of as many as a couple hours of high-stress commuting from the work day.

TIP

If you want to sell the concept of telecommuting in your workplace but think that you'll be left with an empty office when everybody stampedes home to work, don't worry. Many people can't stand the isolation; others lack the discipline to work from home.

Other benefits are financial in nature. True, most companies that allow telecommuting contribute to the cost of equipment, supplies, and phone bills of those working from home offices, and they also have to reimburse the high initial costs of setting up a telecommuting site. However, companies usually find that they save money in the long run. If people are working at home full-time, companies can downsize office space, and even the cost of setting up videoconferencing may be quickly offset by cutting down on the number of phone lines, parking spaces, and break room spaces needed for your in-office work force.

How Telecommuting Works

A few variations on telecommuting exist. First, there's either a full-time or part-time telecommuting situation. In a full-time telecommuting scenario, the employee makes a weekly or monthly office visit. In the part-time telecommuting scenario, a worker works at home two or three days a week and is in the office the other days.

CAUTION

At first look, part-time arrangements might seem better to you because you'll still get significant face-to-face time with your employee. But beware: Part-time telecommuting means financial support of two offices instead of one and an office that sits empty and unproductive for a few days every week.

If an employee is a full-time telecommuter, that person actually might live in another state or even another country. In that case, companies must factor in costs of bringing telecommuters to the office every month or so.

Another consideration is deciding what expenses of the home office the company will cover and what the employee will pay for. Some employees, eager to move into the telecommuting lifestyle, will deal with setting up an area of their home, purchasing ergonomic office furniture, and even paying to install a second phone line. But ongoing costs, such as a computer, phone calls, monthly cost of the second phone line, an Internet account, software, and supplies typically become the burden of the employer. In some situations, employers also are expected to pay a portion of an employee's home utility bill. Whatever the arrangement, make sure that you and the employee are clear about it from the start.

TIP

It might prove easier on your company to arrange for direct billing of some items, such as a second phone line and overnight shipping.

SETTING UP SHOP: THE TELECOMMUTING OFFICE

The existence of various technologies contributes greatly to the success of telecommuting. But each comes with an associated cost—and, in some cases, the time of your Information Services (IS) staff to support it. Be sure that your employee really understands all the things involved in setting up a home office before you both take the plunge.

Some items to consider in setting up a telecommuting situation include these:

- A docking laptop computer so that part-time telecommuters can take their office computer back and forth between office and home easily, negating the need for two computers

- A connection to your company network for access to information and an office e-mail account

- IS support for hardware and software used at home

- A fax machine

- An answering machine or voice mail

- A copier

- A second, faster phone line for Internet access

- Videoconferencing capability

- A two-line phone with hold, mute, and conference capabilities

- Access to an overnight shipping account and materials (consider providing software for generating shipping labels and tracking shipments)

- Supplies of company stationery and envelopes

- Office supplies

- New business cards with home office contact information

TIP

Make sure that your support staff faxes or e-mails documents to telecommuters well in advance of meetings in which they'll be participating by phone.

THE DOWNSIDE OF TELECOMMUTING

But it's not all roses on the road to telecommuting. Although this is a great solution for many employers and employees, and although it can offer clear-cut benefits in terms of productivity and morale, it also has its challenges.

First, your company will face the aforementioned start-up and ongoing costs. This includes the need for IS support for a remote location, which can be complicated and costly.

Be alert to the challenges the employee will face as well. Working at home involves a certain kind of loneliness because socializing and face-to-face interaction is limited or nonexistent. Many people find it difficult to motivate themselves and organize their time with a less rigid schedule and no one looking over their shoulders.

TIP

Take the time to call your telecommuting employee once in a while just to see how he's doing. Make it a policy when you're on the phone with him not to pick up other phone calls or talk with people in the office. This employee deserves a closed-door meeting with you from time to time, even though it's on the phone.

As a manager or supervisor, you'll have your own challenges in overseeing such an employee. You must have great trust in that person and the amount of effort he or she expends every day. You also are less privy to performance issues because you can't observe telecommuters in action. This can make performance reviews much more challenging because you might not be able to cite examples of behavior that you have observed.

Finally, you might face a concern that out of sight means out of mind. The telecommuter runs the risk of sidetracking his or her career. Without being physically present for meetings and other in-office encounters, telecommuters can have a less dynamic presence in the organization. They also run the risk of being left out of certain communications, such as the spontaneous hallway encounter or the lunch with fellow team members at which something important is decided, but nobody remembers to contact the telecommuter.

HOLD THAT MEETING OFF-SITE

Another option for motivating workers without taking the telecommuting route is to get them out of the office now and then for a meeting or other activity. If you remember how you felt when you took a field trip in school, you know the power of getting away from your usual stomping grounds.

TIP

> Does an off-site meeting have to cost an arm and a leg? Not at all. If you hold it over lunch, many restaurants will provide a private dining room free of charge. If the weather's nice, you can simply go to a park.

What occasions work for an off-site meeting? Problem-solving and brainstorming sessions are naturals because new surroundings help you break out of your usual thinking. A quarterly company meeting or any gathering of a larger group of employees is often an occasion to go off-site because most companies don't have a conference room that can accommodate more than 25–50 people.

Whatever the occasion, once you've decided to get away, the next thing is to decide where.

THE RIGHT PLACE

Typical off-site meeting sites are hotel ballrooms, hotel meeting rooms, and conference centers. Those options are fine, and they usually provide the amenities of coffee break service and a business office to help with photocopying and taking phone messages. But if you have the luxury of doing something a little different, try one of these suggestions:

- **Go back to nature.** Head for a nature retreat or the administration building of a large park. These sites often have good-sized meeting rooms for community events. Even better, the beautiful surroundings can be stimulating and make for interesting walks during breaks.

- **Be dramatic.** Rent a local theatre or symphony hall. Some of these ornate older buildings are quite lovely, and the acoustics are great. You can even attend a matinee in the middle of your meeting to support the arts and give your folks a breather!

- **Think art.** Many museums have member rooms or community event rooms available for rent. Once again, the ability to

go schmooze with Picasso on a break can be very stimulating
to good business ideas!

- **Think smart.** Rent some space from a local college, and ask
  a charismatic professor of business or marketing to give a little kick-off speech for your meeting. A college campus setting often provides more attractive surroundings than the
  typical business campus.

- **Get creative!** If you live in California, have a large picnic at
  a winery. If you are located near the beach, grab your towel
  and go! Got a racetrack nearby? Set aside a section of the
  restaurant and conduct your business between horse races
  (but set a limit of $2 per person to bet, please!). Talk to your
  local zoo keeper to see if there's a space in the dolphin house
  for rent.

CAUTION

> When choosing an off-site meeting place, be consid-
> erate to your employees. Make sure there is ample
> parking, that employees know they will be reim-
> bursed for any travel costs, and that the location is
> convenient for handicapped access.

Change More Than Location

One of the greatest benefits of getting out of the office for a meeting is
that it breaks up the everyday routine. With that in mind, also realize
that you'll get the most benefit from this experience if you also try to
provide more than a change of scene.

Being out of the office provides a great opportunity for office workers
to get to know each other in a different way and to break away from
the confines of business as usual. Consider these techniques:

- Leave the hierarchy in the office. (If you're the manager, for
  instance, be sure you're the one to bring the bagels or make
  the coffee rather than leave it to an assistant.)

- Provide time to socialize so that people can chat about themselves outside of their job descriptions.

- Instead of running the meeting yourself, why not ask a bright young employee or group of employees to run part of it? Although you set the agenda, they can moderate, which will make them feel that they have a little bit of authority over the group.

- Even if your main purpose isn't brainstorming, start the day off with a free-form brainstorming session about anything, from the theme for the sales meeting to a new product name. This is a great way to get people involved and contributing equally.

- If you accomplish what you want to do early, give your employees the rest of the day off.

TIP

> You can even take small meetings off-site. Try giving performance reviews out of the office; it can ease tension and make the process more relaxed and informal.

TRIPS AS PERKS

For anyone who has to travel a lot for work, this is no perk at all. But for employees who never get out of the office, an occasional trip can seem like winning the lottery.

Of course, if you can find a business reason for the trip, such as a trade show, a training class, or a visit to the plant to see how your products are made, so much the better. But sometimes a trip is useful just to improve relationships. For example, send the contracts clerk to the New York office to meet the reps she deals with every day on the phone. This will improve their relationships and communications from that day on. Or, let your customer service rep visit a customer site. That also can improve customer relations and even help your staff identify other ways you can serve your customers better.

You can even use trips to scope out the competition. Are you in the hotel business? Send the VP's secretary to a competing hotel in the next city for a night, and have her report on what the competition did right and what they did wrong.

TIP

> To make these trips most productive, ask employees to write a one-page trip report. That will let you see how they've benefited from the trip and make it easier to share any insights they had with co-workers.

THE 30-SECOND RECAP

- Getting people out of the office breaks routine and often stimulates creativity.

- Telecommuting can increase productivity and enhance morale, but it has costs and isn't for everybody.

- Holding meetings outside the office is a great way to motivate people; choose a creative location, and avoid dragging routine and hierarchy along.

- Sending employees who don't have to travel a great deal in their regular work on a trip can provide a motivating perk as well as business benefits.

LESSON 9
Just Go Home!

In this lesson, you learn how to use flex time and other forms of non-traditional working hours to motivate employees.

If you're like 99.9 percent of the working world, your life has become more complex in recent years. You work long hours; you even work on your laptop computer while traveling on a plane or sitting in a hotel room. You're available by pager, cell phone, and Internet 24 hours a day. Oh, and by the way, you might also have a family, friends, and personal interests to juggle. That's not even mentioning those really fun chores like getting your driver's license renewed or your cable TV hooked up in your new apartment.

As William Hazlitt once said, "As we advance in life, we acquire a keener sense of the value of time. Nothing else, indeed, seems of any consequence." Well, take a look at your employees. If you could give them one gift that each and every one would treasure, what would it be? If you guessed time, go to the head of the class.

FLEX TIME: A HOT TREND

Now, we all know that it's impossible to give someone more than 24 hours in a day, and seven days in a week. You can't just go around giving people time off from work arbitrarily—nothing would get done. But you might be able to bend the structure of a typical workday just a bit, and that bending could help out your employees a lot.

A growing trend in recent years, actually brought on by the desire to beat heavy traffic, is called *flex time*. Flex time started when companies wanted to avoid overloaded elevators and long commutes for employees, so they started adjusting start and end times into mini-shifts. Since then, flex time has become even more flexible: Today a flex-time employee's start and finish times are pretty much up to the individual, within some general parameters.

PLAIN ENGLISH

Flex time is a work scheduling system that typically mandates some core hours all employees must work and also requires that the same total number of hours be worked by each employee. However, flex time allows employees to choose their own start and finish times.

THE BENEFITS OF FLEX TIME

So how does flex time help, and therefore motivate, employees? It helps in several ways:

- Flex time helps employees avoid peak rush-hour traffic, making for a shorter commute.

- Flex time allows workers to work when their body clock dictates (those who aren't morning people don't have to drag themselves in at 8 A.M., and those who start to fade by 3 P.M. can come in early and leave early).

- Flex time enables employees to deal with personal demands that don't occur outside the traditional workday, such as day care center schedules, an afternoon class, or personal errands.

- Flex time empowers employees to take charge of their own time and productivity.

- Flex time lowers stress due to worry over personal affairs that aren't being attended to.

CAUTION

In using flex time, be sure to have adequate coverage during non-core hours, especially in positions that involve customer interaction.

Particularly at a time when many households with children have both adults working full-time, this flexibility can be a great boon to balancing job and family.

Current Trends in Flex Time

In 1995, Virginia Slims conducted the American Women's Poll and asked questions about flex time and other factors in working women's lives. A couple of telling statistics came out of this poll.

People were asked what things would help working women balance job, marriage, and children better. Out of eight possible factors, both men and women polled chose men's involvement in chores as the most helpful; both men and women chose more flexible work hours as the second most helpful factor.

When asked if they were taking advantage of flexible working hours at work, 34 percent said they were (a much higher percentage than those taking advantage of job sharing, at 7 percent; part-time work, at 26 percent; working from home, at 8 percent; or maternity leave, at 3 percent).

A whopping 87 percent of women polled said some changes or major changes were needed in terms of workday flexibility in the next 10 years. A still impressive 77 percent of men said change was needed.

It's clear from these results that a lot of workers, both male and female, feel the need for some flexibility from their employers when it comes to scheduling their day.

Flex Time: Take the Survey

Okay, now it's time to take your own survey among your employees to see if flex time is wanted, and if so, what form it might take. Make it anonymous so employees don't feel uncomfortable giving honest answers.

Flex Time Survey

1. What is your most productive time of day?

    a. morning

    b. afternoon

    c. any time I work outside of regular working hours

2. Do you ever find yourself being less productive at your job because you're worried about personal issues outside of work?

    a. rarely

    b. sometimes

    c. frequently

3. How much time do you spend everyday commuting to and from work?

    a. under ½ hour

    b. ½ hour to an hour

    c. over an hour

4. Do you ever take work home?

    a. never

    b. sometimes

    c. frequently

5. If you could work at home one day a week, how would it impact your job?

    a. I'd be more productive

    b. I'd be less productive

    c. I'd get the same amount of work done

6. If your employer would let you work four ten-hour days instead of five eight-hour days a week, would you want to do that?

    a. yes

    b. no

    c. not sure

7. Do you find the balance between your personal and work life …

    a. healthy

    b. slanted too much toward work

    c. slanted too much toward your personal life

8. Do you ever eat lunch at your desk in a typical week?

    a. yes, about once a week

    b. yes, two or more times a week

    c. never

Take a look at trends as you get a few different people to take this survey. One thing I'm sure you'll find is that most answers reveal a desire for a different approach to scheduling working time. The odds are you'll find trends in when people feel most productive (and it's unlikely to be between 9 and 5 exclusively), the inability to provide a balance between work and home life, and openness to nontraditional working schedules.

FLEX TIME AT WORK

Flex time can take several forms. Sometimes it involves variable start and finish times; in other forms, it involves working fewer days with more hours each day. Some companies even allow workers to work longer hours and take extra vacation time to compensate.

TIP

> What are the politics of flex time? Labor unions are typically against it. Apparently, unions fear that employers might force workers to put in more hours per day without paying overtime. If you run a union shop, check with the union before exploring flex time.

Offering flex-time options helps employers recruit and retain workers. And, by providing a mechanism for a healthier balance between personal and work demands, flex time can help reduce employee stress and make people more productive.

HOT FUN IN THE SUMMERTIME

Several companies offer variations on flex time to address seasonal variations in work demand. Some employers adjust hours in summer, for example, to let workers leave in the early afternoon on Fridays. This allows workers to take full advantage of nice weather and spend time with children during their school holidays.

TIP

> Many employers find that throughout a seasonal flex schedule, almost every employee will work through a Friday afternoon now and then because of an important deadline. These workers often report how productive those afternoons are, with no co-workers around to disturb them!

One side benefit of granting shorter workdays in slow business times is that employees are more content to spend longer hours when the business demands it. They know there's a tangible reward at the end of the tunnel.

JOB SHARING

Another flexibility option is *job sharing*. The idea here is that two people share the responsibilities of a single job. Sometimes the two people are husband and wife employees who split childcare and work duties, but not always. Job sharing is often a short-term solution to outside challenges, such as a long-term illness in the family or an employee working on a second college degree.

PLAIN ENGLISH

> **Job sharing** is a team approach to work. Job sharing allows two people to split the responsibilities of a single job so that by each working part-time they complete a full-time job.

Job sharers split not only the job responsibilities, but also the salary and benefits. Because many part-time jobs don't afford benefits, job sharing allows people to work less time at some point in their careers without giving up their position on the career ladder or giving up benefits they might not be able to do without.

TIP

> Thinking of allowing job sharing? Don't forget one great benefit to employers: You almost always have someone to cover that job when one half of the team goes on vacation or calls in sick.

Benefits of job sharing to employees and employers include these:

- Little absenteeism occurs because of family demands because those can be dealt with on off-time.

- Two individuals can develop on-the-job skills and expertise instead of one.

- Job sharers often help each other work through difficult challenges or problems.

- An employer gets two skill sets to call on instead of one.

CAUTION

The last thing you need is a situation where one worker begins placing blame for mistakes or work that doesn't get done on the other. Make sure job sharers understand that they share responsibility for the job being done right. If it isn't, they must solve any inequity between them if the job sharing is to continue.

Of course, you should set a few ground rules when establishing a job-sharing scenario. First, make sure that you have a written job description so that both individuals understand their responsibilities. Also, agree on the split of salary and benefits from the start. Finally, set a time frame for the trial arrangement that can be extended in the future if things are working well. In the event that one employee wants to switch to a full-time job, it's probably wise to designate which of the two people has first claim to the full-time position they are planning to share.

TIP

If the two people sharing a job have unique talents, it's okay to split up the work accordingly. For example, one person might do the phone calling while the other types out the invoices. However, make sure that each is willing to cover the other person's work in the event of an absence.

TAKING LEAVE

Netscape, a leader in the Internet browser market, has a policy that allows many employees to take a four-week *sabbatical* every four years. Should you follow suit?

PLAIN ENGLISH

Sabbatical is a leave without pay for research, travel, or rest. Traditionally, sabbaticals are granted every seventh year to professors at universities and colleges.

Allowing extended time off every few years has clear benefits, including helping to limit the burnout that may result from doing the same work week after week, year after year. Sabbaticals also allow good workers to refresh their skills by reading, taking a workshop, or just relaxing so that they can generate fresh ideas for their work.

Some companies encourage employees to use an extended leave to expand their job knowledge. In that case, this may be a paid leave. For example, let's say you're a magazine publisher and have a manager who purchases printing services. Why not let her spend three or four weeks apprenticing at a printing company to get to know more about the printing business? This makes for an interesting change of pace and broadens the employee's understanding of a key area for your industry.

TIP

Have an employee who loves to travel? Why not let that person spend a month at your branch office in San Francisco—or, better yet, overseas? The employee gets to watch and learn from others doing the same job and also enjoys a change of scenery.

THE 30-SECOND RECAP

- Allowing employees flexibility in their working schedules lowers their stress, decreases absenteeism, and gives them a feeling of empowerment.

- Flex time allows people to avoid longer commutes and to work when their energy level is at its peak.

- Seasonal variations in the work schedule during slower business times rewards employees and motivates them to accept longer work hours during busier times.

- Job sharing is a great way of allowing employees to deal with demands on their time outside of work without losing either benefits or their place on the career ladder.

- Allowing employees to go on leave every few years helps them refresh their spirits and get a new perspective on work.

LESSON 10

Recognizing Achievement

In this lesson, you learn how giving positive feedback and rewarding performance can be great motivators.

It's human nature to pay more attention to the people around you when there are stresses and problems. We reassure each other in times of strife, but when times are good, we sometimes forget to give these same reassurances.

Unfortunately, it's also human nature to thrive on compliments and kudos on a pretty consistent basis. This chapter takes a look at providing positive strokes when things go right—so that successful employees stay motivated—and also giving input so that those who are struggling a bit get motivated to keep at it.

THE IMPORTANCE OF RECOGNITION

Psychologist Eric Berne developed a set of theories of *transactional analysis* that are relevant to this topic. Simply put, Berne looked at all interpersonal interaction as a transaction. A complete transaction involves a stimulus and a response that involves feedback.

PLAIN ENGLISH

> **Transactional analysis** is a theory that states that all interpersonal interactions are basically transactions, each having a stimulus and response.

When employees exert extra effort, this should be a stimulus for you to respond to that work with some form of feedback. If you don't, you're leaving your employees to direct their energies into a void. That lack of feedback can frustrate even the most self-assured individual.

TIP

To be sure you're providing regular feedback, make it a habit to start or end your weekly or monthly evaluation meeting with a positive comment on something that person has done recently.

GIVING FEEDBACK

In my *Merriam-Webster Dictionary*, the first definition of *feedback* is "the return to the input of a part of the output of a machine." Feedback in this sense is the squeal you hear when you get a microphone too close to a speaker. But if you follow the model of transactional analysis, this mechanical definition isn't all that out of line. In an interpersonal transaction, your employee gives you input in the form of effort. You provide feedback by returning output based on that input—that is, a response appropriate to that effort.

PLAIN ENGLISH

Feedback is defined by the *Merriam-Webster Dictionary* as 1) return to the input of a part of the output of a machine or system; 2) response about an activity or policy.

Now, all feedback isn't positive. But at the least, when it can't be positive, it should be constructive. Pure negative feedback without offering suggestions for improvement or solutions to problems is not only cruel, but it doesn't move you or your employee any closer to a solution.

Singing Praises

Let's start with the positive side of feedback. Although you would think that saying nice things is a pretty easy thing to do, several factors or attitudes sometimes keep a manager from giving praise. Here are a few:

- Feeling that people shouldn't need to be coddled.

- Having the attitude that because employees are already getting paid to do a job, and that should be reward enough.

- Figuring that since your manager doesn't compliment you, why should you compliment your employees?

- Believing that good work should be its own reward.

- Finding it difficult to think of anything nice to say to your less-productive workers without sounding insincere.

I'll address all these objections with one argument: Whether or not you personally feel that compliments are necessary, the fact is that most people thrive on them. If everybody did what he or she was hired and paid for, and that level of performance was good enough, your company wouldn't need managers around to motivate the staff. Your job is to get employees not only to do their jobs, but also to enjoy their work and even excel at it. Given that mission, praise is a big part of your job as an effective manager. And, believe it or not, even the poorly performing employee has to be doing something right; if he's not, he should be in another job.

CAUTION

> Providing positive feedback isn't a license to be insincere. People can sense hollow praise. You simply need to develop new radar to be on the lookout for good performance on a regular basis so that your praise can be meaningful.

Of course, the most often-quoted reason for not giving positive feedback on a regular basis is that you're just too darn busy to remember to do it. But consider this: Taking the time to give a little positive feedback each day might save you from taking lots of time to deal with a disgruntled employee—or training a new one—down the road.

PRACTICING POSITIVE FEEDBACK

Not every piece of positive feedback has to be a glowing "Gosh, you're doing a fantastic job!" In fact, feedback can be pretty low-key in both tone and message. To be able to provide compliments on a regular basis, you have to move from the generalized "great job" comment to some more specific comments.

Here are some statements that might help you find reasons to compliment members of your staff:

- Thanks for getting that report in so promptly.
- I can see you're improving in that area; keep up the good work.
- That was an interesting point you brought up in the meeting.
- I got your e-mail and appreciate your getting the information to me.
- You seem to know a lot about this area; I'd like to hear some more of your ideas sometime.
- You handled that situation nicely.
- Your contribution is really making a difference on this project.
- I've noticed that you've been putting in a lot of overtime during the crunch, and it's appreciated.

The point is that just letting someone know you've observed his or her efforts is often compliment enough.

THE ART OF GIVING PERFORMANCE REVIEWS

Now that you're giving positive feedback on a regular basis, let's take a look at the periodic appraisal of performance—called a *performance review*—that has become a staple of business management. Typically given once or twice a year, the performance review incorporates both positive feedback and constructive criticism.

PLAIN ENGLISH

Performance reviews are part of a performance appraisal, or the process of identifying, observing, measuring, and developing human performance in organizations. Performance appraisal was introduced in a study by Carroll and Schneir in the 1980s.

Oddly enough, even good performance reviews can be difficult to deliver. There are a few reasons for this. First, you and your employee aren't used to sitting face to face and talking about him for an hour (although if you're providing good feedback year-round, you may help establish a comfort level for this). Reviews often get into emotional territory, including discussing the relative happiness and satisfaction of the employee, which is outside your typical working relationship. Finally, people tend to obsess about the negative; if 99 percent of the review is good, the employee will hone in on that 1 percent problem area.

But there are some things you can do to make these sessions productive, professional, and positive. Let's get started.

KEEPING TABS

These days, most human resources departments require managers to document employee performance to justify any action that needs to be taken for poor performance. But beyond this basic requirement, keeping notes on an employee throughout the year will help you prepare for an accurate review with specific examples of both good and not-so-good performance.

Get into the habit of making a note when an employee either experiences a problem or does an exceptionally good job. It takes a few moments a week per employee, but if you think about the last time you struggled for two hours over an employee review at year end, you'll see that this will save you time overall.

TIP

Keeping notes will give you fuel for regular, positive feedback. Also, if you keep these notes in a computer file, you can quickly reorganize them and cut and paste them into a written review at the end of the year.

MANAGING BY OBJECTIVES

A good tool both for helping employees to improve their performance and for helping you to organize your performance review is *management by objectives*, often abbreviated to MBO.

PLAIN ENGLISH

Management by Objectives, introduced by Peter Drucker in the 1950s, is a behavior-based system of joint goal setting by supervisors and employees.

MBO is the brainchild of management analyst Peter Drucker, who introduced the concept in the 1950s. Its popularity spread through the books *The One Minute Manager* and *In Search of Excellence*. The core concept of MBO is that a manager and an employee will jointly set goals for the employee. This process enables the manager to assign work to employees in a way that challenges individuals to grow. MBO lets employees understand what's expected of them and allows them to negotiate achievable goals so that they can succeed.

CAUTION

Don't let an employee get away with only easy-to-accomplish goals. Some challenge is good, even for the most complacent employee. On the other hand, don't push this type of employee with too ambitious a challenge—you'll only lay the foundation for failure.

Setting these goals at each year's performance review gives you a framework for tracking and reviewing the employee's activity over the next six months to a year.

Here are some characteristics of MBO to consider:

- MBO is behavior-based, not personality-based. Thus, an employee knows that there is a measurable way to succeed that isn't grounded in vague standards such as attitude or interpersonal skills.

- Because the company needs to get work done, some of the agreed-upon objectives might not be an employee's dream tasks or great career advancers. But be sure to balance the mundane with the challenging, and make sure that the employee buys in to the need for this balance.

- Make the goals large enough that you're not outlining all the detailed specifics of getting the job done; keep them narrow enough that they are clear and measurable.

- If a goal has many variables outside the employee's control, it's important to add that to the description of the goal. For example, let's say that you want an employee to negotiate a new union contract. The goal might be to facilitate the process of negotiating a contract as efficiently as possible, rather than getting a contract signed by a certain day and date, which could be out of the employee's control.

- If you agree to a goal, be sure to provide anything the employee needs to succeed. If she needs funding, resources, or time, discuss these at the performance review before you each agree to the goal.

MBO supports employee self-esteem by involving employees in their own management and presenting them with interesting challenges that will help them further their careers if they succeed. Setting the general goal and trusting the employee to work out its successful implementation is a highly motivating scenario.

TIP

> Be sure that when you agree on a goal with an employee, you also agree on how to measure its success. Specifying quantities, time frames, and quality of work will help you assess success at the yearly review.

BE CONSTRUCTIVE WITH CRITICISM

Of course, there are times either during the year or at the annual review when feedback is needed, but it isn't of the positive kind. You may be surprised to know that many employees get as much of a boost from constructive criticism as they do from praise. That's because constructive criticism, when correctly delivered, tells the employee that you're paying attention. This kind of feedback says you believe enough in the employee to spend your time helping him or her become better at the job.

The key word here is *constructive*. To be constructive, feedback first must point to a problem and then must either suggest a solution or involve the employee in a dialogue about the problem's solution. Here are the ground rules for constructive criticism:

- Reassure the employee at the outset that, in general, you're pleased with his or her job performance, but you want to focus on one area for improvement.

- State that your job is to help the employee succeed.

- Suggest specific things the employee can do to improve.

- Focus on improving the situation, not on excuses for why it exists.

- Don't make light of the situation, but don't spend more time on it than it merits. A lengthy discussion about a small problem can leave the wrong impression entirely.

- Listen.

Did you notice that last one? I hope so. Listening to the employee's input on why the problem exists is vital to providing useful feedback. We're not talking about excuses here, but about hard information on why this area is difficult for the employee and what you can do to help.

REWARDING EXCELLENCE

When an employee does great things, you should make a point of doing something more than commenting on it or including it in a review. Sometimes, based on the employee's capabilities, seniority, and company structure, reward takes the form of a promotion. But when a promotion isn't possible or appropriate, you can use other forms of recognition to reward excellence.

PROMOTIONS MOTIVATE

One of the most rewarding things for me as a manager was wholeheartedly endorsing an employee for a promotion and then getting approval for that promotion from senior management. Promotions are a tangible way to reward good performance in terms of salary, title, and responsibility.

But to be strong motivators, promotions must be given judiciously. If they come too quickly from you, they can cause future frustration when the next manager promotes more slowly. If a promotion comes before an employee is ready to take on greater responsibility, you can be setting him up for failure. If a promotion is delayed too long, you may be organizing that employee's going-away party as she sails away to a more rewarding workplace.

Use these guidelines in handing out promotions:

- Don't promote one person too frequently. Too many easy promotions begin to lose their meaning.

- Make sure a promotion fits in with organizational goals for this individual and provides the type of training and challenge that will continue to make this person valuable to the organization.

- Make sure you understand your employee's long-term career goals, and that the promotion fits those goals.

- Be sure that the employee is ready for the promotion and that he understands the responsibilities and expectations that go along with it.

- Don't discount a lateral move if that might be useful in broadening the employee's skill set to help her reach her eventual goals.

- Do announce a promotion right away, and specify the reasons for it. This ensures that others have a clear understanding of the new responsibilities of this person, as well as a model for what kinds of behavior can get them a promotion in the organization.

AWARDS AND GOLD STARS

Of course, it's not always possible, nor appropriate, to give a promotion for great job performance. In those cases, you should begin to stockpile some other ways of recognizing people.

Here's a list of just some of the types of things you might do:

- Authorize the employee and significant other to go out to a nice restaurant and expense the cost.

- Implement an Employee of the Month program, and provide a set of perks to go along with it. These might be a designated parking space near the office entrance, a feature article in the employee newsletter, or an extra day off.

- Buy a stash of gift certificates or small presents, and leave one on an employee's desk with a thank-you note for a job well done.

- Send flowers.

- Take the employee out to a nice dinner.

- Post the employee's picture on the company Web site. This boosts the employee's morale and shows customers that your company values having good employees to serve them.

- Give two tickets to a sports or artistic event (many companies have seats for sporting seasons for clients that might be available to employees now and then).

Whatever reward you give, it's important that everyone understands that there was a specific accomplishment for which it was given. That stops people from accusing you of favoritism if one person gets a few rewards. Also, being clear about what sparked the reward tells other employees what will win them the same prize and thus motivates them to emulate that behavior.

TIP

Give rewards on a bell curve. That is, if one employee isn't exactly the star player, but she does do something above average *relative to her abilities*, give her a reward. Constantly rewarding the best people can be demotivating, so spread the rewards around and strike a balance.

THE 30-SECOND RECAP

- Recognition is an important motivator and should happen on a consistent basis.

- Transactional analysis theory suggests that every interaction is a transaction, and your response to good performance should be positive feedback.

- Feedback should be sincere and frequent.

- Performance reviews provide an opportunity for both positive feedback and constructive criticism.

- When an employee does something exceptional, you can reward him with a promotion or some other appropriate sign of recognition.

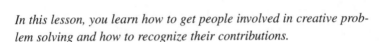

Lesson 11

Involving People in Innovation

In this lesson, you learn how to get people involved in creative problem solving and how to recognize their contributions.

Allowing people to contribute to innovation in the workplace is a two-way street. Employees feel empowered and appreciated when their ideas are solicited and, even better, implemented. Employers get solutions and products that keep them on the leading edge in the marketplace.

The Foundation for Organizational Innovation

Innovation itself isn't clearly defined. When you get a great idea and nobody acts on it, was it an innovation? Not really. Innovation involves both the development and the implementation of an idea. If you implement an idea and it flops, people don't often refer to it as an innovation, although by strict definition, it probably was. Innovation generally relates to new ideas that are implemented successfully.

Innovations can be small ideas for doing a job better, or they can generate new products that are a perfect fit for the marketplace. But it's generally acknowledged that some of the most successful companies support innovation at every level of their operations.

Social scientists have studied *organizational innovation* carefully over the years. Although nobody has discovered the magic pill that makes innovation happen, there are some good ideas about what kind of work environment fosters innovation.

PLAIN ENGLISH

Organizational innovation consists of planned efforts by groups of people to develop and implement new ideas.

The first (and most obvious) point is that innovation occurs in contexts that motivate innovation. That motivation can come in the form of financial incentives for great ideas or acknowledgement of one's part in the generation or implementation of those ideas.

TIP

Interestingly, studies have shown that incentive pay is a weaker motivator than simple recognition for one's contribution.

One organizational theory is that organizational segmentation and bureaucratic procedures constrain innovation. In simpler terms, the more you're divided from other areas of the company, and the more layers of process separate workers from implementing their actions, the less innovative the organization is.

The following is a list of various conditions that studies have shown to foster innovative behavior:

- Appropriate resources

- Communications across workgroup lines and among workers with different viewpoints

- Some level of uncertainty and the ability to focus attention on change

- Workgroups that are cohesive and resolve conflicts in a way that integrates creative people into the mainstream group

- Access to role models and mentors who are good at innovation

- Low turnover

Now, you may not be able to change your entire workplace to mirror this list, but you can at least look for ways to implement these ideas in your own group.

SOLICITING IDEAS

Most people have the ability and the potential to be creative and innovative. They need only the structure that encourages it.

On an individual level, look for or create settings to solicit ideas from each of your employees. Let people know that ideas are listened to and that, if successful, their contribution is recognized and rewarded.

On an organizational level, one of the most important things you can do to get innovation going is to support an open communication model.

OPENING UP YOUR COMMUNICATION MODEL

Sometimes individuals come up with great ideas all on their own. But more often, the really good ideas come from group involvement. You can encourage that interaction by opening up communications, not just among those who think alike, but especially among those who totally disagree.

If you have created a good team environment among your people, they won't be afraid to bring conflict out in the open and resolve it. That's the foundation for a good communications model. When people with different ideas or opinions aren't afraid to express them, you discover different ways to approach a problem or question.

CAUTION

Although your own ideas may be very good, don't make the mistake of thinking it's a good thing when everyone in the group follows your lead all the time. They must know that you are open to having them disagree with you.

Take the time to ask people what they think about a problem or idea, even if it's not their area of expertise. Gathering different perspectives on a problem is key to innovative solutions. When you do get ideas from people, avoid these innovation-killing phrases at all costs:

- We tried that before, and it didn't work.

- That's not really your department.

- I appreciate your input, but it's out of my hands.

- Why don't you just focus on your job and leave this to me?

- That sounds way too risky.

- We've never done anything like that before.

Finally, encourage communication among different groups in your organization. They might have very different takes on an issue, and striking a logical balance between disagreement and cooperation can be tricky. But it's out of this balance that true innovation usually surfaces.

BE OPEN TO CHANGE

All the encouragement of open communication and soliciting of ideas won't amount to a hill of beans if your organization is afraid of implementing change. Even the most creative employee will stop offering ideas when nothing ever changes.

True innovation comes when companies are willing to take risks, when there is a model for change, and when people are willing to make a leap of creativity and faith.

One key to this risk-taking attitude is to clearly define what problem you're trying to solve with innovation. A great idea for its own sake is less likely to be implemented than a great idea that solves a specific problem. The problem becomes the motivator for the organization to make changes.

TIP

> Recent studies have found that organizational change is most effective when it is multifaceted, affecting several subsystems and areas of the organization.

As much as possible, support a future-focused organization, one that is aware that change is inevitable and that looks for proactive ways to set a vision for the best future possible. When employees sense that structure and are encouraged to contribute to that vision, they are much more motivated to work harder and stay the course to see the outcome.

CREATIVITY TECHNIQUES

Okay, you've done what you can to examine your communications model, you've opened yourself up to change, and you generally support an environment that fosters innovation. Now, what specific techniques can you apply to get your people in a creative mood? First, let's take a look at what creativity is.

WHAT IS CREATIVITY?

At its most basic, creativity is simply the ability to create something. But most people add another element to this definition. The *Blackwell Encyclopedia of Management*, for example, defines creativity as "the generation of ideas or products that are both novel and appropriate."

The novelty in this definition relates to the originality or uniqueness of the idea. The use of the term *appropriate* refers to the way an idea relates to the need at hand, solving a specific problem or fulfilling a market need.

Some people consider creativity to be a personality trait. Others have said it is a process. In the context of this latter characterization, anyone can be creative by being involved in a creative process.

USING BRAINSTORMING AND SYNECTICS

The creative problem solving process, devised in the 1950s, basically is a fancy name for what we all recognize today as brainstorming. Brainstorming consists of certain elements:

- Listing

- Forced relationships

- Delayed judgment

- Generation of large quantities of ideas

Missing out on one of these items could result in less effective brainstorming sessions. So, effective brainstorming sessions involve long lists of ideas that are written down. No idea is thrown out, and no judgment on an idea's value is passed until late in the process. Finally, relationships between ideas are used to work to a final solution.

Synectics is somewhat similar to brainstorming, but here the focus is on use of metaphor and analogy. The idea behind synectics is to try to look at things in a completely different way. If the typical response to a budget overrun is to cut back on staff, turn the problem upside down and consider what would happen if you added staff.

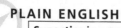

PLAIN ENGLISH

Synectics is a process using analogy and metaphor to look at things differently, thereby generating novel ideas.

In a business setting, the use of analogy or metaphor can take the group's thinking out of the workplace and help you see ways in which you would treat a problem in another setting that just might work at the office. Here's an example of how to use synectics:

> **Problem:** We can't seem to get customers to send in survey cards telling us how to improve our customer service.

Analogy: When I'm trying to get my small children to do something, I make it into a game.

Solution: What if we held a contest? Every time somebody submits a comment, that name is entered in a contest for free products.

ACKNOWLEDGING CONTRIBUTIONS

So now you've got everybody in your company creating and innovating like mad. You might have set up bonus incentive programs to reward contributions to innovation. But don't forget one other very important thing: Acknowledge individual and group contributions. Studies have shown that *intrinsic motivation* is much stronger than *extrinsic motivation*. That is, personal motivations such as interest in an activity or personal challenge are much stronger than outside motivations such as money.

PLAIN ENGLISH

Intrinsic motivations are interior, including personal challenge and involvement. **Extrinsic motivations** are outside of oneself, such as financial or career rewards.

Acknowledgement of effort supports intrinsic motivation. You are publicly giving praise to someone for having achieved a personal goal or having been involved in and committed to an idea.

Acknowledgement can take many forms, such as these:

- Publicly thanking people in a larger group meeting
- Making sure that a story about the achievement shows up in the employee newsletter
- Copying the employee on a memo or e-mail to senior management that commends his contribution
- Noting the contribution in the employee's yearly performance review

Whatever you do, do not take credit for others' contributions. First, it's unethical. Second, it usually gets found out. Third, your credit should come from the fact that you manage people in a way that allows them to be their most creative and productive.

THE 30-SECOND RECAP

- Innovation is a way for companies to stay ahead in the market and for employees to feel vested in the company's success.

- Innovation occurs in an organization that supports risk-taking and is willing to accept change and open communication.

- Communication involves openness about conflict and its resolution, as well as the interchange of ideas among people with different perspectives.

- Techniques for bringing out creativity include brainstorming and synectics, or the use of analogy and metaphor to place the problem outside the workplace setting.

- Never forget to acknowledge employee contributions of ideas or solutions.

LESSON 12
Providing Challenge

In this lesson, you learn how providing challenge involves balancing goal-directed activity and goal fulfillment to keep employees motivated.

Think about the last time you started a new job. Everything was new, and you might have felt overwhelmed by the challenge of taking on the unknown. Now think about a job that you left because you had learned everything there was to learn and were bored to tears when you came into work every day.

These are examples of the two uncomfortable ends of the spectrum of challenge. Neither too much nor too little of a challenge feels right. Your job as a manager is to strike a balance for each of your employees. This chapter tells you how.

UNDERSTANDING GOAL FULFILLMENT

Much of the time that you're working on a project, you're performing *goal-directed activity*. You are actually enjoying the anticipation of accomplishing your goal because it's tantalizingly just out of reach. Once you accomplish your goal, you are in the *goal-fulfillment* phase. Often, this phase is somehow less satisfying than the goal-directed phase because the challenge is gone.

PLAIN ENGLISH

Goal-directed activity involves the tasks you perform in the expectation of reaching a goal. The **Goal-fulfillment** involves the attaining of a goal.

In fact, if you think about the life cycle of any endeavor, you'll see that you usually generate much more energy toward the beginning than at the end. That's the power of expectancy.

THE EXPECTANCY THEORY IN ACTION

What you experience when you're more excited at the beginning of a project than you do when you're nearing its end is what the *expectancy theory* is all about. At its core, the expectancy theory claims that people's actions are based on their expectations. Most people do things not for a reward, but for the expectation of a reward; they put in effort because of their hopes and dreams rather than for tangible payoffs.

PLAIN ENGLISH

The **expectancy theory** states that people perform tasks in expectation of success.

To understand the expectancy theory, consider this: Although you work hard on a major project for 200 days out of the year, you don't get 200 rewards. You work those 200 days in the expectation of a successful product launch or a great big bonus at the end of the project. You might not even get a bonus, but you work because you imagine you might.

Now, the motivation gained from expectancy isn't constant; it involves some cycles. For example, look at your favorite sports team. If the players are in the fourth quarter and are 20 points ahead, they might just start getting sloppy. If they're in the fourth quarter and are 20 points behind, they might give up. The best games happen when there's a good chance that either side might win. Then each side is deeply involved in the anticipation of winning rather than the surety of winning or losing.

TIP

> Not convinced about the expectancy theory? Just ask yourself if you've ever left a game in the last inning. You left not because your team was losing, but because their win was so sure that it just wasn't interesting anymore.

This tendency to lose motivation as success seems imminent was documented by David McClelland and John Atkinson in the concept of what they call a 50 percent curve. When the probability of success is near zero, motivation is low. When probability of success approaches 50 percent, motivation increases. Finally, when probability of success gets higher than 50 percent, motivation begins to fall off.

CHALLENGING EMPLOYEES: IT'S A BALANCING ACT

Therefore, the key to challenging employees is to make sure they are neither too complacent in their work nor too unsure of their ability to succeed. Success must seem possible, but not a sure thing.

CAUTION

> There's a difference between keeping your employees on the cutting edge of challenge and getting them edgy. Make sure they succeed often enough to feel the good side of challenge.

Read over these tips for using expectancy theory to strike a balance between goal-directed and goal-fulfillment activities:

- If you know that workers have passed the 50 percent probability of success on a project, encourage them to redouble their efforts; you can even raise the stakes a bit. Praise their efforts to date, and then define success a little more aggressively. (Be sure, however, that if you promised rewards at the initial success milestone, you provide them.)

- One theory states that three things must be available for expectancy: Someone believes his efforts affect performance, believes that performance determines outcomes, and assigns a value to those outcomes. Pay attention to the second item: If the outcome isn't attainable because of market factors or a lack of resources, motivation goes out the window.

- Allow your employees to share in the larger vision of the company. This plays to the nature of people to be motivated by what they imagine to be possible. Then make sure they understand that their actions relate to the success of that vision.

ASSIGN AN INTERESTING PROJECT

One of your jobs as a manager or supervisor is to distribute the workload among your staff. Your first priority is probably to get the work done. But right up there on your priority list should be to distribute that work in a way that challenges and stimulates your employees.

Now, some businesses are in constant flux, and new opportunities to take on projects abound. But other workplaces are pretty consistent, and the people you supervise might be required to do the same repetitive task every day. It's trickier to provide stimulation in this situation, but it's not impossible.

Even a factory worker with one assigned task to perform all day long might be able to help assess a new piece of equipment. Although a secretary must type and copy documents all day, you could give her a research project now and then. Look for unique activities to intersperse throughout each person's work week, and you'll go a long way toward providing a challenging environment.

CAUTION

> You should be aware that some people absolutely love routine and get scared to death when asked to take on something new. Learn to recognize those people, and give the interesting projects to someone else.

TRYING ON DIFFERENT HATS

Whenever somebody takes on a new responsibility, it's a challenge to his ability to learn and absorb new situations. That something new could be an entirely new type of work he has never performed before. It also could be a kind of activity he has done, but in a new setting, with new people, or with more responsibility or authority.

Remember, your job is not to assign brand new activities on a daily basis, which would be inefficient in getting the company's business done. Your job is to find activities that balance new challenges with routine work. This ensures that an employee finds enough stimulation in the work to enjoy the workplace.

Here are some examples of challenging situations that can be incorporated into any employee's work life:

- Ask a clerical worker to learn how to perform research on the Internet. Although he has done research before, he might never have used this tool, so he would be in a learning situation.

- Invite a factory worker to be involved in a project to improve working conditions in the plant. Although she might never have been part of a committee working with management, she knows conditions in the plant firsthand and can contribute that expertise in a new setting.

- Invoke a skill you know an employee has but that he or she has never used in a business setting. Let's say, for example, that Sally often gives talks on bird watching to a local nature club, but has never given a business presentation. You can have her transfer her existing skill to a business setting. Although she faces a new challenge, she'll have enough confidence about the skills involved to be pretty sure she'll succeed.

- Say that one employee has purchased printing services for years for your company. Now that you have more work to produce and need additional printing vendors, you might give her the job of meeting with possible vendors and giving her recommendations.

TIP

> Sometimes managers hesitate to assign more responsibility to people because they're worried that those people will fail. It's always best to trust an employee to perform well, but if you have any doubts, work along with the employee on a project and observe his performance before letting him fly solo.

SKILLS BUILDING 101

Offering challenges to employees isn't purely to keep them amused on the job, although that is important to attracting and retaining good employees. Through challenging new situations, employees stretch themselves, learn new skills, and exhibit abilities that help you and them see the next logical step in their career paths.

You can develop many types of skills with special projects, including these:

- **Technical skills.** High-tech skills are the wave of the future, so consider letting your employees learn to use the Internet, a software product, or a new piece of equipment.

- **Management skills.** An employee can acquire management skills if you assign him or her the responsibility to train another person, to supervise another person's performance, or to give input for the budget for your department.

- **Communication skills.** Good communication is key in moving up the career ladder. Assign projects such as writing a proposal, speaking to a group, or giving a demonstration.

- **Interpersonal skills.** When you put an employee in with a different mix of people, he'll get to flex his interpersonal skill muscles. Put a worker on a committee with people from another department, or have her go along with a salesperson on a sales call. Although she's not in sales, she might be able to help the salesperson explain the features of the product to the customer better.

TIP

Part of providing opportunity for advancement is spotting skills that are transferable to other roles in the company. Is your assistant good in building relationships? Maybe there's a fit for her in sales or customer service.

Listen Up!

When you're trying to think of ways to provide challenge and variety to your employees, it's always important that you factor in their goals and interests. That's not hard to do if you simply listen to what your employees want.

Try these questions to discover what types of new situations or challenges might be best suited to your employees:

1. How do you feel about working on projects with other departments?

2. Do you enjoy picking up new skills? What skills do you think you would like to learn?

3. If you could find ways to use your existing skills in new ways, what might those be?

4. Are you interested in managing other people?

5. Do you like training or mentoring others in work that you're familiar with?

6. Do you enjoy familiar routines? Why?

7. Are there any activities you definitely do not want to be involved in (public speaking, managing people, traveling, and so on)?

8. What would be advantageous to you in having more authority over other people?

9. Do you have suggestions about ways in which you could do your job differently to improve productivity or allow you to be more creative?

PROMOTING FROM WITHIN

Although most companies profess to promote from within, some companies don't do so in practice. Why? In some cases, it's because it takes work on a manager's part to groom employees to add skill sets that make them promotable—some companies don't support managers spending their time that way. Some management types want only those with experience in higher-level jobs to do those jobs. Then there are some people who have prejudices. The sentiment "He's a clerical worker, and someone at that level could never handle this kind of responsibility," is more common than you like to think.

CAUTION

Never, ever let yourself hold an employee back because he or she is invaluable to you in a current role. Absorbing the headache of letting someone good move on and training a replacement is a fact of life for any manager. And eventually, anyone held back time after time will find the front door and walk.

So what are the motivational benefits of promoting from within? People have a natural tendency to want to grow and change throughout their lives. They work through stages of physical development, emotional development, and intellectual development. No matter how much you may want to keep people in the jobs they have today, they eventually will want change, and if you don't provide it, another employer just might. People like strides in their development to be recognized and rewarded.

TIP

Some companies give more credence to outside training than on-the-job training. If taking classes or getting a second degree will help management consider an employee in a new light, encourage people to try that route to promotion.

If people believe that effort and a broader skill set will win them the reward of growth through promotion, it provides tremendous motivation to work hard and try new things. If taking on new challenges isn't going to lead to growth, why bother? Meeting challenges for challenge's sake works for a while—maybe even years. But at some point, people want their efforts recognized.

THE 30-SECOND RECAP

- People often are motivated not by success, but by the expectation of success.

- If success is impossible or assured, motivation goes down.

- New challenges motivate employees because of the promise of possible success in a new endeavor.

- Challenging employees can help them acquire additional skills that will benefit both the company and the employees' career goals.

- Talk to employees to understand what kinds of challenges they are interested in.

- Promoting from within, as a policy, makes workers aware that taking on new challenges can lead to more than praise.

LESSON 13
Share the Success!

In this lesson, you learn how sharing the benefits of success can moti-vate future effort.

When all is said and done, you and your co-workers are working to achieve success for the company. You do that so you will continue to have jobs, but also so that you will see some reward from all your hard work.

You can reward employees on a day-to-day basis with paychecks, par-ties, gifts, or recognition. But when the company's ship comes in, don't forget to invite the employees to the party on the dock. That's what this chapter is all about!

OWNERSHIP ISN'T JUST FOR OWNERS

Some companies forget that employees want to feel part of something bigger than their own daily responsibilities or their own careers. Because many employees are not involved with setting the course or overall vision for the company, those who are involved sometimes don't credit employees with major accomplishments. This is a big mistake. People have a natural inclination to want to belong to some-thing bigger. And because their work makes your success possible, it's only right that you make them feel involved.

This investing of employees in your company's success goes beyond making them feel warm and fuzzy, or even sharing financially in suc-cess. If people feel involved in where the company is headed, they are likely to stay with the company longer and view their own efforts as more important in the scheme of things.

Share a Piece of the Action

As noted in other parts of this book, personal motivators such as challenge and involvement have been found to be more motivating than outside motivations, such as financial reward. But in the case of sharing the wealth in successful times, you're really appealing to both kinds of motivations: You're making employees feel involved by including them in the financial rewards.

Sharing Profit

Profit sharing falls under the category of variable compensation. This means that the amount you'll pay out to each employee varies depending on the performance of the company.

TIP

One benefit of having a profit-sharing program is that you can vote to reduce the profit-sharing margin if times get bad as a way of offsetting losses rather than laying off employees.

Three types of profit-sharing programs exist: cash, deferred, and a combination of cash and deferred. Cash plans pay a cash bonus either quarterly or annually, based on company financial performance. Deferred plans place an employee's payment into a tax-deferred fund. A *deferred profit-sharing plan* is basically a retirement fund. The combination program pays both a cash bonus and a payment into a retirement fund. 401(k) plans are a form of profit sharing in which an employee can contribute a portion of his pay into a tax-deferred fund, and the employer matches the contribution.

PLAIN ENGLISH

Deferred profit-sharing plans make payments into a tax-deferred fund. As long as the employee does not withdraw any funds, she does not pay taxes on the income.

Profit-sharing plans *vest* over a period of time. When vested, funds are available for an employee to access. The most common time period for vesting is seven years. This is a stepped process, with a certain percentage of the fund vesting each year until the 100 percent point is reached.

PLAIN ENGLISH

Vest   To grant or endow with a particular authority, right, or property.

Profit-sharing and 401(k) plans are very popular with employees. A 1999 survey by The Profit Sharing/401(k) Council of America (PSCA) shows that 87.4 percent of eligible employees participate in a profit-sharing or 401(k) plan. Average employee deferral contributions are around 5.5 percent of their salaries. On average, companies contribute 4.9 percent of their payroll to these plans.

TIP

For more information about these programs, visit the PCSA Web site at www.psca.org.

STOCK OPTIONS

Companies that have gone public can grant stock options to their employees. Stock options are basically shares of stock granted to an employee at a certain value. In future years, after the options vest and are available to the employee, that employee can exercise them by selling the shares at the current market value. The employee receives the difference between the option price and the current market price.

Companies can also set up a system by which employees can purchase additional stock options out of their paychecks with regular deductions.

Stock options are a great motivation for staying with a company because one has to wait a certain number of years to exercise those options. If an employee leaves the company, the options don't go with him.

TYING BONUSES TO SUCCESS

Most bonus programs also offer complicated formulas that relate the size of the bonus to the financial success of the company or the work unit. The benefit of tying a bonus into performance comes when employees believe that their own work performance can impact the overall performance of the company and, therefore, their bonus amount.

Although you might not be able to affect the percentage of salary an employee receives in the form of a bonus, you can impact the perception of whether individual effort results in company success. You can do that in several ways, including these:

- Keeping employees informed about company initiatives and successes on a regular basis.

- Initiating a two-tiered bonus structure that rewards both overall company performance and workgroup performance. This way, if other groups fail, your own group's success can still save the day—and the bonus—for your people.

- Setting group goals that are measurable and related to profit, such as number of units produced, new accounts opened, or an increase in the number of customer inquiries processed.

 TIP

Senior management's communication with employees is very helpful. Suggest that senior managers hold a quarterly lunch with a handful of employees picked at random from different departments. Management can listen to their input and express appreciation for their efforts.

Spread the Good News!

When your department or the company as a whole achieves a success, it's vital that management inform employees as soon as possible. Employees often feel cut off from the larger initiatives that a company is involved in, such as negotiating mergers or going public when the first they hear of it is on the 6 o'clock news.

Some companies make the mistake of not following up after a big employee initiative. For example, if you've launched a new product, it probably took the efforts of hundreds of people from research and design, marketing, manufacturing, and so on. Yet, many companies don't share sales results after the launch, so people don't really know whether their efforts paid off. They always hear if the product falls flat on its face, but they should also be told about a nice big order that came in from a major customer or an award that the product received.

Here are some mechanisms for sharing the word when success hits:

- Use a company Web site or newsletter to announce the news.

- Hold quarterly company meetings, and designate one section of the meeting just to announce good news.

- Throw a party, or send out a special bonus when an unusually important goal is achieved.

- Print buttons that say "We did it!" and distribute them in paycheck envelopes with a brief description of the accomplishment.

CAUTION

Some employers hesitate to share financial information or future plans with employees because such information is confidential. By asking employees to be involved in keeping this confidence, you express trust that makes them feel valued. Be sure to warn employees when information is not to be shared, though.

NOW GET OUT THERE AND MOTIVATE!

Well, that's the last chapter of this book, and the last theory I'll offer you about motivating people. But I can't resist one more list! Here are a few thoughts I'd like to leave you with:

- Remember, the very fact that you bought this book (and read it straight through!) means that you are a caring and concerned manager. Give yourself a pat on the back for the effort you're expending on motivating your staff.

- Often, simply being more alert to how your employees feel about or react to a situation helps you find the solution. Let your people know you're in tune with what's happening to them and how it makes them feel. Whether you can do anything to change it or not this time, that recognition means a great deal.

- Think back to the very first chapter and remember that people go through phases of motivation, that different things motivate different people, and that they're not always the same things that motivate you.

- There is no replacement for day-to-day leadership, honesty, fairness, and integrity. All the gifts, parties, promotions, and bonuses in the world can't replace these.

If you implement many of the recommendations in this book, over time you'll find you have a more motivated work force and that your own job is more pleasant and fulfilling. Good luck!

THE 30-SECOND RECAP

- Making people feel involved in larger company successes reduces turnover and makes employees feel part of something bigger than their daily tasks.

- Profit-sharing and 401(k) plans reward employees for company and department financial performance.

- Tying bonuses into financial performance encourages people to put in effort for which they see a direct monetary reward.

- There are several ways to spread news about company successes, including newsletters, Web sites, and company meetings.

GLOSSARY

cognitive dissonance   A condition that arises when there's a conflict between one's perception of oneself and the way the world perceives one.

decision teams   Teams that function primarily to make decisions. An example would be a committee that is formed to review flex-time policies at a company.

deferred profit-sharing plans   Plans that enable employees to make payments into a tax-deferred fund. As long as the employee does not withdraw any funds, he or she does not pay taxes on the income.

distance learning   Any structured learning that takes advantage of communication media, such as computers and videotapes, to allow learners to study in a remote location but under the guidance of an instructor or educational institution.

e-commerce   The buying or selling of anything online through the use of the Internet.

equity   The state or condition of being just, impartial, and fair.

ergonomics   The design and use of furniture and other tools to reduce physical strain on employees.

expectancy theory   A theory that states that people perform tasks in expectation of success.

extrinsic motivations   Motivations that lie outside of oneself, such as financial or career rewards.

feedback   As defined by *Merriam-Webster's Dictionary,* feedback is 1) return to the input of a part of the output of a machine or system; 2) response about an activity or policy.

flex time   A work-scheduling system that typically mandates some core hours all employees must work; also requires that the same total number of hours be worked by each employee. However, flex time allows employees to choose their own start and finish times.

goal-directed activity   The tasks you perform in the expectation of reaching a goal.

goal-fulfillment   The attaining of a goal.

inequity   An imbalance or lack of justice.

intrinsic motivations   Interior motivations, including personal challenge and involvement.

job sharing   A team approach to work. Job sharing allows two people to split the responsibilities of a single job so that, with each working part-time, they complete a full-time job.

maintenance factors   Things about a business that contribute to a healthy business climate, but that do not cause it. For example, a clean lunchroom may not motivate good performance, but if it's not clean, people will complain about it. In that sense, cleaning the lunchroom becomes a maintenance factor.

management by objectives   A behavior-based system of joint goal-setting by supervisors and employees; introduced by Peter Drucker in the 1950s.

Maslow's Hierarchy of Needs   A theory stating that human beings have an innate order, or hierarchy, for the things they want. When one level of this hierarchy is satisfied, they move on to the next.

mentor   A trusted counselor or guide. Mentors impart knowledge to others based on their real-world experience.

motivation   An incentive, an inducement, or a stimulus for action. A motivation is anything—verbal, physical, or psychological—that causes somebody to do something in response.

organizational innovation   Planned efforts by groups of people to develop and implement new ideas.

performance appraisal   The process of identifying, observing, measuring, and developing human performance in organizations. Performance appraisal was introduced in a study by Carroll and Schneir in the 1980s.

performance reviews   Part of performance appraisal.

sabbatical   A leave, without pay, for research, travel, or rest. Traditionally, sabbaticals are granted every seventh year to professors at universities and colleges.

Socialization Needs   One of the stages of Abraham Maslow's Hierarchy of Needs; Socialization Needs involve personal fulfillment from social interaction.

synectics   A process using analogy and metaphor to look at things differently, thereby generating novel ideas.

tchotchke   A Yiddish word that has become a catchall phrase for small gifts or giveaways—such as notepads, pens, or key chains—that companies give to employees or customers.

team   A group of people with a common goal who use the unique strengths of each member and the combined strengths of the group to achieve that goal.

telecommuting   The practice of allowing employees to work from their homes, taking advantage of various technologies to connect them to other workers and information; also called *telework* or *flex work.*

theme   In terms of a party, a theme is a subject or topic of discourse or artistic expression.

transactional analysis   A theory that states that all interpersonal interactions are basically transactions, each having a stimulus and response.

vest   To grant or endow with a particular authority, right, or property.

work teams   Work teams have to coordinate individual efforts on a day-to-day basis to perform tasks; a space shuttle crew is a work team.

INDEX